Let Children be Children

What's the Hurry?

Malavika Kapur

वत्स
LET KNOWLEDGE SPREAD

Published by
Renu Kaul Verma
Vitasta Publishing Pvt Ltd
2/15, Ansari Road, Daryaganj
New Delhi - 110 002
info@vitastapublishing.com

वत्स is an imprint of Vitasta Publishing

ISBN 978-93-86473-30-1

First Edition 2018
MRP ₹399

Editor Papri Sri Raman
Cover and layout by Somesh Kumar Mishra
Printed by Vikas Computer and Printers

Contents

PART III

CHILDREN AND SOCIETY

PART IV

CHILD HIMSELF

PART V

WHERE DO WE GO FROM HERE?

Preface

I began working as a clinical psychologist with children and adolescents very early in my career in Scotland, in Manipal and in Bangalore. Till mid seventies I was using a clinic-based approach. My horizon expanded when I ventured into schools in 1976.

In India, half the population consists of children and adolescents. The mental health facilities offered them are scarce.

Beginning of the Community Mental Health Movement at the National Institute of Mental Health and Neuro Sciences, Bangalore was my first experience of approaching the schools with the aim of sensitising teachers to mental health of children.

To my surprise, they were neither interested nor motivated to help children by promoting their psychosocial development.

Their sole interest was in promoting academic performance.

We were talking at cross purposes. This led me to seek solutions to the problems for the Indian school children encountered. My programmes kept expanding, based on failures or successes along the way.

First was the School Mental Health Programme for urban schools, training in counselling for teachers covering about 10,000 children.

The realisation that rural schools were worse than urban schools made me move into the rural schools, couple of decades later. First one was a programme involving 1,200 children in rural schools where actual intervention was carried out through child-centered 'play way' method which resulted in dramatic improvement in overall development including intelligence and creativity in the children as they discovered the joy of learning.

Even more impoverished were the tribal children. A programme with 800 children proved to be very successful. Currently the programme is run on limited scale in government schools in Bangalore and ten tribal schools and one high school for SC/ST children in HD Kote, Karnataka.

In addition, bridge programmes have been carried out for the children from disadvantaged homes, admitted to good schools under the provision of RTE (Right to Education–2009). Children in India are surrounded by adversarial and non-congenial situations. These are posed by adults, mostly unintentionally and sometimes deliberately for personal gains.

As a child psychologist, I have been deeply distressed by the callousness of adults adversely affecting development of children knowingly or unknowingly. Initially, I jokingly described this compilation as 'Laments of an Indian Child Psychologist'. My thoughts and experiences may be applicable to children in other parts of the world as well.

The only ray of hope that I hold in this dismal world of our children is that much of these are unintentionally caused.

If we sensitise adults to the impact of their actions on the children, it may lead to a conscious course correction. This is where our hope lies. In view of the last chapter on the silver linings in the scenario, I have decided to change the title to a positive one.

The book examines three areas which impact children: home, school and society, before moving to the child's world, spotlighting situations at home and outside, including school compromising the child's development and mental health due to the very nature of parenting.

Home

- Children who have different temperaments they are born with.
- There are mental health issues like attention deficit, learning problems, emotional problems and behavioural difficulties which the parents believe are deliberate and react to with verbal and physical punishments.
- There are parents, siblings or family members who stress out children. We, often, cannot even imagine the reasons. It may be something inconsequential to us adults but bears great importance in the mind of the child.
- The real or psychological joint families who provide either support or create stress from multiple directions.

School

- The very school system we so strictly abide by in India, is a source of misery.
- The school is a place where there is no consideration of individuality, creativity and imagination. Mere rote learning is encouraged. The teacher is regarded as the sole reservoir of knowledge while in reality, it may not be true at all.
- Quality education that promotes the overall psychosocial development of the child is mostly absent in our schools.
- In the private schools, sacrificing the child's creativity on the altar of the Syllabus god, with its mindless overburdening work is the norm.
- In the government schools, it is a case of total indifference and neglect of children.

- Needless to say, all the teachers believe that they are doing a great job. This is why we cannot provide quality education to our children unless we change the mindsets of our teachers and parents.

Society

- The major evil force in childhood is deliberate action of adults for personal gains that destroys childhood. Examples are child abuse of varied nature at home, school and society in general.
- Aggression towards children is the key theme. There is manipulation of children through advertisements and reality shows which cause loss of innocence.
- Technology too has a key role to play in this. It is not known how much the impact of mobiles, video games and other technologies may harm the child's brain and its normal development. Harmful effects from unknown sources pose grave dangers to the young. Even when proven to be harmful, the genie is already out of the bottle and the damage is already done!

Thus, we have children forced to live in the badlands at home, in school and society. Who is there to support them to grow up normally as they deserve to? In addition to dealing with the psychological impact, I have included case illustrations of children in India in this book.

Laments should not remain a lament. I have, therefore, also suggested how positive changes can be brought at home, school and the society. In this book, the child is always in the focus. Resiliency of the child is the best protector. The book deals with difficulties faced by children at multiple levels and offers a holistic solution. It is not a panacea. It is only a beginning.

Speaking about the child as s/he seems clumsy. Alternating

the two is a nuisance. Calling the child 'IT' is a worse crime. In the entire book I have used 'He' to stand for the human child, needless to say a girl child too. All the names of the children in the vignettes are fictitious while the case contributors are real.

The narratives in this book are based on empirical data. No work is worth considering unless it involves outcome evaluation, especially in this kind of work. Large number of corporate houses and NGOs do good work in schools, but these are hardly ever evaluated. The present work contains insights using quantitative (based on psychological tests) and qualitative (based on narratives of children, teachers, parents and the field staff), thus providing a holistic view of problems and their solutions, especially in the school settings. After all, that is where most children are or will be in the future.

June 2018

Malavika Kapur
National Institute of Advanced Studies
Indian Institute of Science Campus
Bengaluru 560012

Acknowledgements

I thank all those who have generously contributed to this compilation of experiences, especially the lay counsellors of Child Guidance Centre, Prasanna Counselling Centre, Bengaluru. Special thanks to Harish Aatreya, Sheela Kamath, Sindhu Karanth, Rajalakshmi, Aarthi Rao, Mithila Sharma, Anitha Sudheer, Veena Suresh of CGC, Prasanna Counselling Centre and Namitha Kumar of NIAS and for their contributions. All of them have contributed the different vignettes given in the text. My special thanks to Rajalakshmi, who shared the chores of copy editing and proof reading. I owe deep appreciation for Ajai Nair for his positive suggestions. I am truly grateful to Dr Keshav Kumar of NIMHANS for his line drawings in the last several chapters. Owe much gratitude to Renu Kaul Verma and Papri Sri Raman of Vitasta Publishing Private Limited, New Delhi for their support to this book as it evolved.

Let us together take an oath to make our children happy. I am truly grateful to my parents, Leela and Shivarama Karanth for giving me the gift of a gloriously happy childhood and I do wish that all children be this fortunate.

PART I
CHILDREN AND HOME

1

Child Development and Child Rearing

OVERALL, THE development of a child, any child anywhere in the world is a multidimensional process and consists of physical, intellectual, language, emotional, social, moral and sexual development. These form the seven strands of development. These need to occur in an integrated manner for every child. Even a child like Wilma Rudolph or Coy Mathis.

There are various stages (phases) in all the domains of development. For example, from birth of the newborn to three months there is a kind of physical development typical to that age, such as moving limbs, trying to reach out and grab and so on. At six months it is different and may consist of rolling over or crawling. At nine months the child may be sitting or even attempting to stand, at times even walk.

The same wondrous phases of development occur across months and years as well as across domains. Take for example, how the infant starts with babbling and ends up speaking. From diffused emotional expressions, specific emotions such as joy or anger may emerge. From infancy to about twelve years of age, overall healthy development is very crucial. If there are deficiencies or uneven or deleterious environment, normal development is compromised.

For years it was thought that teaching languages to children as young as three was futile. Research findings indicate quite the opposite. Longitudinal studies by Harvard University confirm that learning additional languages increases critical thinking skills, creativity and flexibility of the mind in young children. The brain, like any other muscle, functions better with exercise. Learning a language involves memorising rules and vocabulary, which helps strengthen that mental muscle. It is now believed worldwide that at pre-school stage, children should be introduced to at least four languages. Understanding this is crucial for India, a multilingual nation. Households and schools especially need to rethink on language studies and change teaching dramatically to be able to reap advantage for a 21st century India. Mental maths is another subject not given sufficient importance, especially in the age of calculators.

Reasons for Healthy and Deficient Development

Some believe that it entirely depends on the environment while others firmly believe that it is determined entirely by heredity.

To paraphrase one of the famous behaviour psychologists, BF Skinner who believed that only the environment matters, he, in fact, famously declared, 'Give me a child, I will shape him into anything'. While there are others who believe that even intelligence is totally determined by heredity. However, both positions are wrong though both are true. Both heredity and environment play equally significant roles in promoting or hampering development. There is not just black and white, development is a grey area influenced by various and most inputs.

Unfortunately, be it psychologists or politicians, a person tends to support the view that suits him/her.

For example, if intelligence is determined by one's heredity, there is no need for promoting education for the poor, backward or disadvantaged children. In India, education has been the prerogative of the wealthy and people of higher castes, while 'mass education' has been promoted in recent times with no 'political will' to push it. No change would be possible if the claims of those who believe only in heredity were true, while all changes are possible if the predominance of environmental influences happen. But reality is in between the two as both are equally important.

In India, one of our earliest story streams tells us this. Vishnusharma's *Panchatantra* stories are more than two thousand years old. These begin with a king who has three lazy and uneducated sons. When all teachers fail, the king calls Vishnusharma to educate his sons, and thus was born India's most famous story book. If heredity had been a factor, the king's sons would have been born wise and learned.

Everyone believes that he or she is an expert when it comes to bringing up children. The aim of this chapter is to attempt to highlight what is known about children's development. This chapter, therefore, dwells on three time-frames and related thinking on children's development.

1. What was known about child care in India 1,500-2,000 years ago in Ayurveda and such ancient healing systems? What do they tell us about how to bring up children?
2. In the last century, how did Western thinkers examine the way we view our children?

3. In the last 30-50 years, the above ideas have undergone major shifts due to advent of developmental psychology.

We need to know all the popular thinking in all the three eras to understand our children.

There are generally four stages of intellectual development children go through, up to the age of twelve years according to the Swiss psychologist Jean Piaget. The teenagers and adolescents are similar to adults in their cognitive (intellectual) abilities, of course, with some variations due to specific push and pull of adolescence. I am going to describe four stages with metaphors to signify these four developmental stages in brief, this will be elaborated upon in Part IV.

1. **Abhimanyu** - This stage covers foetal development
2. **Scientist in the Crib** - Birth to three years
3. **Wandering Scholar** - Three to six years
4. **The Victorious Adventurer** - Six to eleven years

In all the above stages there is all-round development. These simultaneously occur in the physical, intellectual, language, emotional, social, moral and sexual domains. For the normal development in all the domains, the care of the child is essential.

First, we should determine at each stage what does the child require and what appropriately needs to be provided by the caretakers in the right kind of environment? This is what we are going to examine now in each of the four stages.

Those familiar with the epic *Mahabharata* would know that Abhimanyu learnt his war strategies while he was in his mother's womb. In contrast, Western thinkers/psychologists have believed that the child is born with his mind 'full of blooming buzzing confusion at birth' to quote the eminent psychologist, William

James. This also puts the onus of teaching the child everything on adults as the child arrives in the world knowing nothing.

The ancient treatises of *Kashyapa Samhita* and *Charaka Samhita* describe the foetal development from the point of conception itself. Not only there is rapid physical development at the foetal stage, awareness of pain and pleasure at three months, consciousness at four months, emergence of mind at fifth month and intellect at sixth month. Eighth month is considered an unstable period where there is imbalance in both, the energy systems of the foetus and the pregnant woman.

Kashyapa Samhita, in view of the above knowledge, recommends excellent regimen of physical and psychological care for the foetus, pregnant woman as well as the nursing mother. This is considered *Kaumarabhratya*—care of the child.

Traditionally, in India, care starts much before the baby is born. Both the parents, especially the mother, is advised about diet, cleanliness, behaviour, rituals to be followed. Her mind should be happy and peaceful. She should entertain good or pious thoughts and see only pleasant people and experience soothing events.

These instructions are given as it is believed, whatever happens to be her physical and mental state—these strongly influence the foetus/infant. Many of the social rituals too are based on the above observation. To provide such emotional, physical and social supports, a special status and some rituals are recommended during pregnancy. In the traditional home, the young woman during much of her pregnancy and during the first year after the child's birth is taken care of in her maternal home. This notion of all-round support for the pregnant woman and nursing mother is desirable scientifically and psychologically as preferred practices in many countries, including in India.

This is almost absent in Western cultures. These days, this gap is somewhat alleviated by hired help who are trained in the care of the infant and in maternal care. These days some awareness through research has emerged in the Western scenario.

Detrimental effects of environmental pollution, smoking and alcohol consumption on the maternal and child health too have been reported. Alcohol, drug residues have been detected in the newborns if the foetus has been exposed to these during the mother's pregnancy.[1]

Other studies have shown effect of changes in the maternal state in that of EEGs (Electro Encephalography) of the foetus. The effects of music and pleasant or unpleasant noises on the foetus have been noted.

Thus, it is universally accepted that the yet-to-be born foetus has continually developing brain, body and mind and is constantly in interaction with psychological and physical environment.

The 'clean slate' and 'blooming buzzing confusion' statements have been completely demolished by contemporary developmental psychologists. There are empirical studies that support the notion that the newborn arrives totally equipped physically and psychologically to grow and learn, facilitated by the healthy interaction with the environment while the inhospitable or uncongenial environment may hamper normal development.

Thus, it becomes necessary for us to understand that given the right kind of environment, all children will thrive.

---

[1] The famous book on developmental psychology by A Gopnik, A Metzoff and P Kuhl have come with two titles: The American edition, *Scientist in the Crib* and the UK edition, *How Babies Think*, in 1999. The author has drawn inspiration from this book.

Within a week or so, the newborn observes his environment, tracks lights, recognises mother's face and voice. S/he can differentiate mother's face from a mask and does not like to look at it. S/he observes more things in the environment than what we give him credit for. He expresses his unhappiness, hunger or discomfort through his cries. His happiness and contentment is communicated through smiles and laughter. An observant mother can actually know if the cry is because of hunger or sleep.

Present day research supports the contention that development starts in the foetal stage itself and this can be promoted, providing right kind of environment. Thus, in all the developmental domains infants and children actively seek stimulation soon after. But the children of course, vary vastly. These individual differences determine how they interact with the environment. Different children may respond to the same environment differently.

Relating to the World

1. How does s/he understand the world?
2. How does he psychologically and socially respond to the world?
3. How does he interact with it through behaviour and language/communication?

Some simple descriptions of how the child makes sense of the world and interacts with it:

How does the child understand the new world he is born into? Alison Gopnik and co-workers discovered that the newborns can differentiate human faces and voices from other sights and sounds in the environment. A month old can respond by sticking the tongue out if you stick your tongue out at him. The innate skills of mimicking an infant comes with, is indeed astounding.

Learning about Objects in the Environment

Infants prefer certain shapes and colours and like to look at these for a long time. They prefer certain shapes and moving objects. In the olden days, various coloured and sound-making objects were hung above the cradles. Now 'mobiles' or attractive hanging toys are hung above the cribs. They keep listening to noise and watching the moving objects endlessly.

Piaget's pioneering work divided cognitive development into four phases. A six-month-old reaches out for a ball if it is shown to him and would repeatedly drop it and enjoys when it is retrieved and given to him. But if he cannot see it, he stops the game. What is out of sight is out of mind. However, by the ninth month, he is able to look for a hidden ball. Soon he is able to play 'hide and seek' as well, with great excitement.

By the time he is three years old, he is able to look for the cause—but understands the cause differently than adults. There is an old story about a crow, which thought that it broke the huge branch of a tree when it sat on it. Young children attribute cause to events that occur at the same time. The child trips and falls accidently at the time the door bangs loudly. The child believes that he fell because of the banging of the door.

As young children do not speak and tell us what they are thinking, we believe that they do not understand anything. They can differentiate long and thick lines from short and light lines, similarly with voices and noises. But these can be only understood by experimentation and observation. Some research shows that though children start speaking by eighteen months to twenty-four months, they understand the speech pattern much before that. Noam Chomsky believes that children are 'prewired' for language acquisition at birth. Thus, the natural language the child is exposed to at six months builds a basic foundation for language acquisition.

> An example is about Prerana, a musician and her young child. She used to keep him on her lap while giving music lessons. At three months he would scream in distaste if a student sang tunelessly and badly. If the student sang well, he would go to sleep. At nine months he was naming the 'ragas' and 'talas' asking his mother to sing. Around that time if they played a tape of classical raga when he was crying, he would vary his crying coordinating with the taped music. This, of course, is a family of three generations of musicians.

In the initial years of my work with rural children, what we normally did was to take a huge supply of drawing books, crayons, craft materials like gum, scissors, cello tapes, scraps of fabrics, coloured papers and so on. Along with these we also took some basic group game materials such as carrom boards, snakes and ladders, ludo, tennicoit rings, balls and bats. On one occasion, we arrived at lunch time. We left the materials in the school and told the children, we too would have lunch and come back and distribute the materials and teach them the rules of the games.

When we came back, the children had opened the box with tennicoit rings and were already playing with the rings. We told them, 'we will teach you the rules'. They said, 'we already know the rules'. I simply smiled and asked them to show me the rules. Each of the ten children there had developed a new set of rules and were playing and thoroughly enjoying the different games with the same object. This was a revelation to me—that 'our rules' are fixed and focus on cultivating a particular set of skills. The innovative approach to the tennicoit allowed the children to use the same object in multiple ways. Often rules 'kill' creativity and innovation. We discovered, if given to children to play with, they will create manifold ways of putting some basic material to use.

In the same school, we found children rubbing the old faded black board with leaves of Datura plant which abound around the school. They were using these leaves to darken the black board. Children taught us through their traditional stories how the various animals behaved, how Shaman had taken possession and so on. These children were highly innovative. We made a list of over fifty games they played regularly. They were the storehouses of riddles and proverbs, giving insights to their rich culture.

Language Development

Children vary in the time they start speaking. Some start at ten months, while others at two or three years. What is important to observe is if he understands when spoken to. Some children start very late, at five years, but catch up quickly and speak fluently thereafter.

But as highlighted by human development scientist Lois Bloom, children have the innate ability to learn languages. Most Indian studies show that our children speak multiple languages with ease, while we as adults have much difficulty in learning new languages. Once children start to speak, their vocabulary increases at a very rapid pace. No adult can compete with them in the speed of acquisition of new words.

Language and Cognition

Language and Cognition have very close relation. When one understands the world of objects/people in a particular way, language helps us in communicating this to each other. As we grow up, language and cognition are inextricably mixed.

A child of eighteen months moves around a great deal, touches and plays with everything. This is very essential for development of cognition and language. When we say 'no' and 'stop' we are hampering their development. They should be protected from danger but should be allowed to play as much as they want. **Play is the most important tool of promoting child development.**

This raises the question, what is the role of parents? And of teachers?

When the children are two-three years old, the parents want to know if they should be sent to 'play home' (where, in many places, play is not permitted) or nursery school. They insist that the children be taught reading, writing and maths. Teachers too want to achieve, thus colluding with parents.

At two, three, four or five years, it is completely unnecessary to teach them school-related skills. Before the child is physically or mentally ready, making the child learn scholastic skills is WRONG.

A child who cannot hold a pencil with two fingers is made to write alphabets endlessly. No wonder after five minutes of this torture he runs away! *Why 'torture' the child when her/his hand and finger coordination is not developed, these tasks given under the guise of teaching is actually physically harmful.*

A simple example, when the child is able to sit but unable to walk as yet, should we force him to walk, holding his hands or putting him into a walker? If given two to three more months, he will joyfully take his first steps and walk soon enough. Before the child can sit, should we force him to sit? What is the hurry? Why harm the child this way? This approach is psychologically damaging too. Why should copying alphabets be considered enjoyable? If you give a crayon (big enough to hold in hands) and a large sheet of paper, the child will explore the activity joyfully. He will draw the lines, makes circles or simply scribble or even make a totally messy unrecognisable picture and will say 'This is Mummy'. This is what a child should be doing.

All the fine motor and gross motor movements and eye-hand coordination will eventually lead to the skills that are needed for writing. What is the hurry? With a drawing book and a box of crayons or a lump of clay or plasticine he could happily spend hours and days, never getting bored.

The main drawing is the ball and the smaller structure of the two on the top is his mother.

When a young child does not like the task, he obviously

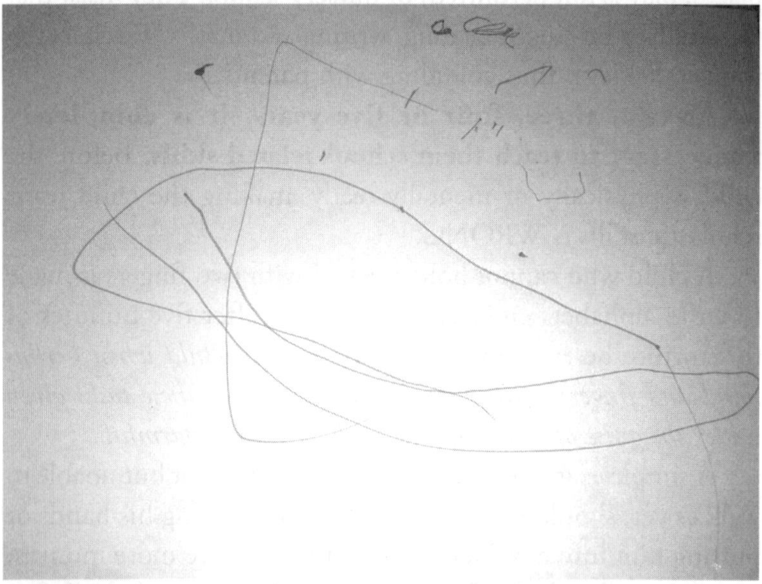

The sample of one-and-a-half year old Varchasvi's drawing

does not understand the concerns of the parents. But are the parents needlessly concerned? If the child can play, it is the beginning of the learning process. When the child draws something and tells you that is what he means, why can you not accept it? The meaning belongs to him not to you, as seen in the above drawing.

Have you ever wondered why a child loves scribbling and hates writing? If you tell him to read he refuses but if you tell him that you will tell him a story, he will enjoy it immensely. He looks at the pictures of a book when mother reads to him or mother herself enjoys reading, he understands that reading is a joyful activity.

Most parents and teachers make reading appear to be a dreary chore and not an enjoyable activity. When the child is yet to walk, should you make him ride a cycle? When he is ready, he will enjoy it and learns in no time at all.

Around three years, the child wants to experiment with all his daily activities, eating, bathing, brushing hair, wearing clothes and shoes. But often parents believe that they are too young to do these and insist on doing everything for them. Not only are parents depriving them of the joy of self care and independence, but also render them incapable of it as they grow older. How will he learn these necessary skills of self care if you don't let him? Once again, these promote fine-motor, gross motor skills and eye hand coordination.

You want him to learn reading, writing and maths when he is physically and mentally not ready, but deprive him of learning essential skills of self care when he actually likes to learn. Once a child gets used to others doing everything for him, it becomes hard to break these habits later on. In India, the mothers or other adults take pride in doing everything for the child. I have seen even ten-year olds being fed, given bath, dressed up and so on. 'Otherwise he does not do it!' My explanation is that 'You made it so!' Instead, if the parents empower the child in self care, they will enjoy the parenting much more.

Up to now, physical and cognitive development has been described. What about emotional and social development?

There are stages of emotional development up to the age of three. All children are not alike. They have their own temperament or emotional predisposition that they are born with. There are several theories of temperament of children in the West. In the *Samhitas* we talk of *Triguna* as temperament. These are *Satvik* (happy, cheerful), *Rajasik* (irritable, quick) and *Tamasik* (slow and laid back). One infant, soon after birth, may be placid, feeds and sleeps well and is generally easy to take care of. Another may be very cranky, crying all the time, not feeding or sleeping well and is very hard to take care of. Another one may be slow and lethargic. We need to recognise that each child is a person with distinct temperament characteristics. My own work supports the use of this framework for Indian children.

Because of these differences the child starts responding differently to people and objects in the environment. The healthy interaction between the mother and child is dependent on the child's and mother's temperaments and personality characteristics. An easy child may be managed well by an irritable mother but if the infant too is irritable, caretaking becomes a battle of wills! Both parents and teachers treat all children as being equal in their emotional predisposition. *Adults need to be sensitive to individual temperaments of children.*

In addition to the above there are distinct phases in a child's emotional development. American psychologist Harry Harlow studied infant monkeys and discovered that the babies cuddled up to the mother not just for feeds but also for warmth and comfort. For the first few months of life human babies need physical proximity and affection to thrive. The British psychoanalyst, John Bowlby, highlighted the negative impact of early maternal deprivation. He reported that the infants, children in orphanages without maternal bonding, grew up to be listless, aloof and not interested or curious about the environment.

By the time the child is nine months old, he needs attachment and bonding with the mother or caretaker. He can understand her absence and feel the separation. This is the age when children cling to their parents and get upset when they are not around. This continues up to three years. In the West, parents believe in keeping the young children physically distant to encourage independence later on in life. In India and other Asian countries, there is much physical bonding between the caretakers and young children. The children also sleep with their parents for a longer duration.

In the Indian traditional society, babies are given traditional bath and oil massage by experienced persons. This practice is now being given up in modern nuclear families. The physical stimulation provided by massage is seen as a very important promotive activity for the young ones. In the West, this has come into vogue to treat high-risk babies. Most babies enjoy the massage and afterwards feed and sleep well. It also appears to promote physical development as well as bonding.

In this phase, the child likes to move out, mix, play and talk with other children. He is skilful in learning languages and uses the language for communication. They are forever curious, asking questions endlessly. Most adults feel it is a waste of their time to answer these questions. Adults fail to recognise the reasons behind these questions. It is not just curiosity, but they have other questions as well. I will illustrate this with some anecdotes:

> A three-year-old once looked at the statue of the cosmic dance of Nataraja and asked me some questions after very closely observing the statue. This is an icon most of us are familiar with, Shiva trampling and killing the demon, apasmara purusha (symbolically representing ignorance).
>
> *She Asked:*
>
> Why is he trampling on the child?
>
> Why is the child's mother not doing anything to protect her baby?

Where is she? What will she do?

This child identifies herself with the trampled demon, who does look like a baby. Then she is concerned that the mother, who should be the protector, is not doing so. There is also empathy for the weak being. There is anger against the mother for not protecting him. Then there is the belief that such bad people should be punished.

If this little girl had not asked these questions, I would not have gained entry into her inner world. Such a wonderful and complex understanding of a statue, which we appreciate only as a piece of art! Do we as adults have so much empathy?

Alison Gopnik gives an example: After a frustrating experiment and failure in writing her thesis she came home and wept. Her little daughter came and stuck plaster on her legs, hugged and kissed her and said, 'You will be better soon, don't cry'. She knew what to do when her mother was upset, because this is what her mother does when she is upset.

Alison's pain vanished at that moment.

We always underestimate children.

When I told my little grandson on the beach,'Look at that bird' he said,'It is a sand piper'. I had already assumed that he lacked knowledge. It is only by talking to them that you understand what deep thinkers children are.

> In a summer camp for the age group of 10-12 years, the story of 'The Giving Tree' was read. The group was happily listening, identifying themselves with the little boy who was loved by the tree. Later when the boy began exploiting the tree till it became a stump, the merriment of the children was transformed into a silence. No sound even after the story ended. When feedback was asked – a unanimous voice came out – 'Sad!!!' Empathy had shifted from the boy to the Tree.

A three-year-old child asked his parents where he was in their marriage photo album. Parents struggled to reply. Seeing them baffled, the child comforted them, 'I was there in the air, as a bird, on the tree. I was somewhere, may not be visible to all'.

> A six-year-old boy asked why people die when they meet with an accident. The adults around him went on explaining to him the details of what all happen as a process. The boy repeated they should not die, when they fall under any vehicle. He explained his theory to make the adults understand his viewpoint—'There is "death" following every man, always staying at a man's back (nobody knew where he picked this concept from). When he falls down, his "death" dies first. When his "death" dies, how can the man die?' None of the adults around him at that moment had any answer to satisfy him.

Children keep asking questions. We need to be patient, keep answering them. If we do not know the answers, we must find out and give the answers to them. Children can be our greatest teachers. To paraphrase the well-known educationist, Prof Yashpal Sharma, 'Learn from children what to teach them'.

When we lack imagination and creativity, how can we teach children? We draw something and ask children to copy it. Copying is an act that kills imagination and creativity. If you give ready, realistic toys to children there is less scope for creativity. If you give an empty box, an empty carton, a piece of paper or cloth and ask him to make whatever he wants, you will see each child making different and new things.

I gave an assignment to Anganwadi teachers in a class on promoting play in a preschool. I told them to give children an empty box of matches or an empty ice cream cup or a cloth and observe what the children can convert these into. The Anganwadi workers were astounded with the number of objects produced by these children. They said, 'We never knew these children are so bright!' Children also learn by observing other children. So, playing with other children is important. It also teaches them how to play cooperatively, taking turns and without cheating. Thus, playing with other children promotes pro-social behaviour and moral development. They can learn right values at home and from friends.

Children are good at imitation. They learn many behaviours by imitation. If a child observes on the television a doll being broken, when given the same doll the child destroys it instead of playing. This ability to imitate can be encouraged by good behaviour of adults and children. *Viewing of violent and destructive behaviour may induce children to learn by imitation such negative behaviours quite often.*

When children watch television, they may understand it differently. At times,they even misunderstand and get upset or scared. Some age-appropriate programmes are essential for normal development, but very few television channels provide this at present.

At six years, they start understanding cause and effect in a very practical and concrete manner.

Philosophy of life according to Jivaka

Jivaka, the five-year-old philosopher, pointed to his mother's abdomen and said,
'This is my old home!'
He showed the present home where they lived.
'The future?'
'The sky where I go where I go after I die!' he added.
'But mother …the sun is my permanent and last home because everything comes from it and goes back to it.'

Five-year-old Jivaka's mother gave birth to his sibling. He had wanted a baby sister. He watched in distress his mother having labour pains for a few hours before the baby was born. The newborn turned out to be a boy. Since Jivaka wanted a sister, the family wondered how he would react to this event. He appeared relieved and said,'I am glad it is boy. If it were to be girl she would later on, when grown up, suffer from pain like my mother did!'

> **Analysis of fickle-mindedness by Jayant**
>
> Once Jayant was walking on a line on the floor. When asked about it he said, 'I want to walk on ropes, when I grow up. So, I am practising now itself to make it easier later on. In reality, I was very interested in trains. Now I am becoming fond of cassettes. Similarly, later on, I may get other interests than rope walking!'
>
> —*Contributed by Rajalakshmi*

What adults lack in the combined thinking and feeling is evident in this child's statement so succinctly expressed. I believe that if only we can get into their world we will find what great philosophers they are!

Around the age of six years, children are sent to school. With that their world dramatically changes. It is their first exposure to the real world, away from the secure and familiar home environment. Every experience is a new experience.

School can be a wonderful adventure, or it can be a jail or a cage. Their thinking is often superior to that of adults. By nine, they are able to indulge in abstract thinking. They now use adult-like logic. Children of this age are ready for adventure. They welcome new experiences. Providing these to enrich their exposure and experience is in the hands of the teacher. This is the age when a child can think logically and understand the world around. This is the right time to start academic skills.

In the Hindu Brahmin tradition, the 'Upanayana' ritual is meant to be performed around six to seven years of age or thereafter. This is the age when the child is ready to learn to read, write and do maths. Education begins later for other castes.

In India, education at the age of 5-6-7 can happen in two different ways:

One is the high-pressure model where there is 'play school' and necessary classes where reading and writing are taught rigorously, endlessly and monotonously to the detriment of the child's development. In all the classes it is more of the same.

In India they have a ritual of *Vidyarambha (Haathe Khari* in Bengal) in many communities. The child is taught in a repetitive and routine manner. *Instruction is on 'How it is to be copied or repeated'.* No one bothers to even think how it can be made interesting.

This is where play way method can come to help in teaching of scholastic skills, especially to 80 per cent to 90 per cent of children in India in rural, tribal or urban government schools. All the research shows that almost no learning takes place in these play-schools, primary schools. A fifth grader has only the reading and maths skills of a second grader. Poor infrastructure, poor pupil-teacher ratio, teacher and pupil absenteeism and poor teaching methods seem to be some of the causes. But children from disadvantaged homes who have illiterate parents add to the problems faced by the first-generation literates.

For urban upper and middle-class children, schooling has become like 'child labour'. Teacher is the only person to instruct and it is assumed that a child has to learn only by rote. *These children have to go to school early, feeling sleepy at times on empty stomach, just with milk. Then they sit in the classes for about eight hours, come home to face tuition and homework and sleep at 10 pm or watch television serials.* Where is the time to play and relax?

In the vast majority of Indian schools, the teachers are either absent or have poor teaching skills. They are indifferent and even show disdain for the children they teach. They label these children as idiots, useless or un-teachable and make no efforts to reach them. Jayakumar Anagol, an educationist, has sadly declared that, 'the only teaching aid Indian teachers use is a stick'.

This is the crucial period of schooling when instead of providing challenging, exciting environment, our children—rich or poor—are provided uncongenial environment.

Play that promotes their overall development is absent in their lives.

To Summarise

The newborn arrives in the world fully equipped to understand and relate to the world. This needs to be recognised. Stimulation and interaction is essential for overall development. The infant/toddler needs physical nearness and warmth of the caretaker. Once he is secure in his relationship, he is ready to move into the outside world. Then he should be permitted to explore and be adventurous. Up to the age of three, he needs a bonding and secure mothering, but after that he needs freedom. Once he goes to school, the teacher needs to empower him to learn but not impose on him to learn by rote in a meaningless way. *Play is the natural method of promoting overall development.*

Positive Approach to Child Care – Some Pointers

To paraphrase Shivarama Karanth, a renowned author, what a child deserves is like a small laddoo and not half a laddoo. A child is not a piece or a half. He too is a complete person in a simple pattern of everything, which an adult is familiar with. A child is nearer to natural norms and stranger to the social norms; whereas, we adults have moved away from nature in our zeal to merge with the social norms. A child thus appears totally ignorant to an adult.

1. Normally we deal with a child with negative instructions. For example:
   'Don't run!'
   'Don't do this!'
   'Don't go there!'
   We could easily change these into **positive instructions.** For example:
   'Please go slowly/carefully'
   'Could you please do that?'
   'Please come/stay here'.

The child always is in a ready state to do 'something'. When we say in a negative tone to stop him from doing something unwanted, the child will end up doing what we say not to.

2. Children love challenges, whereas adults are scared of them. They work to meet their challenges. The challenges are their learning tools as well as process. Children try to explore what challenges (interests) them by knowing, thinking, talking and working about with it. This is how they learn. We can understand this aspect if we observe their activities with patience and attention.

3. In today's rat race, rarely do all the members of any family meet. Every family should make it a point to spend time together for some activity on a daily basis. This allows the family to have **some quality time.** But this activity or talk should not be about home work or watching television. It should be an activity, may be dining, playing or even singing together. At present parents hardly know their children and their real potential, other than their academic grades.

4. Involve children in the household activities also in a gradual and phased manner. Let a corner of the

household **responsibility** be theirs. It would help them to know that the family matters to them and learn to handle the tasks independently. They can share, starting from a very small responsibility of the home. They feel trusted along with being at par with all other members of the family. You will wonder at their ability to manage things.

5. **Entertainment** (outside home), humour, indoor/outdoor games, travel, be it short or long may be considered to be some of the ways to strengthen the bond among the family members. Please try to keep gadgets as well as school-related topics away from your conversation.
6. When a child is unable to meet the scholastic expectations of his class, the first thing to check is if the child's vision, hearing or the motor coordination is alright. If the child is fairly intelligent, he may even have learning difficulty or disabilities. He may require some professional help, if the other problems are all ruled out.
7. Please observe and **appreciate** your child's good behaviour, before blaming them for their bad behaviour. Your appreciation encourages, motivates the child to repeat similar actions. Criticising and blaming the child all the time brings his self esteem down and appreciation builds up this self esteem.
8. Sometimes parents may have had their ambitions or dreams to achieve something but have been unable to do so because of a variety of reasons. If yes, please look back into your own past to see if you are trying to fulfil

them through your children. Your children may have their own dreams. Let them work for their choices.

9. Meeting all demands of a child is not the sole expression of your love towards your kids. **Setting the limits** is also equally important. Make them understand their limits and practise to be within that limit.

10. Accept a child's demand/s at the first request, if you think the child needs it and you can afford it. Please be firm with your decision, even if it is a NO, irrespective of the child's tactics. Explain to the child the reasons behind your decision, if the child stays polite. If he gets into tantrums, ignore the tantrum.

11. Parents/teachers should understand that a child may have limits beyond which he cannot achieve and try not to expect beyond a certain limit. They should not contribute to lowering a child's self-esteem.

12. Most of the teachers are parents too. Their children are more stressed than their students, as they are expected to perform better than other children. This aspect need to be recognised, especially by teachers who are parents. They need to be consciously less demanding of their children, preferably along with other students.

13. A teacher may allot one session a week to revise the week's teachings. Let it be through the children bringing out what they learnt during the week, in the form of drawing, painting, crafts, play, drama, mimes, dialogues, speech etc. **without adult interference**.

14. Each child is born with one's own special attributes. Nurture and respect those abilities also. Let us overcome our self-imposed glorification of only scholastic abilities,

totally neglecting all other skills. A teacher, along with the parents, can contribute to a great degree in this area.

In the next few chapters we shall elaborate on what other experiences children are exposed to, such as television, video games, advertisements, mobiles and other gadgets and their impact on development. The bad influences at home and school will be highlighted with anecdotes.

2

Parenting Fault Lines

WALKING ON a sword's edge or joyful parenting is your choice. Some simple points to remember are:

The United Nation's Convention on the Rights of the Child (UNCRC) considers all below 18 years as children. It gives a detailed account of what are the rights of children.

These can be divided into three groups: Addressing the child directly, Addressing the government and to the adults in general. There are 40 articles. Some are cited below.

Article 1: Everyone under 18 years of age has all the rights in this convention.

Article 2: The convention applies to everyone whatever your race, religion, abilities, whatever you may think or say and whatever type of family you come from.

Article 3: All organisations concerned with children should work towards what is best for each child.

Article 4: Governments should make these rights available to all children.

Article 6: You children have right to life. The government should assure that you survive and thrive.

Article 12: You have the right to say what you think should happen, know what decisions adults are taking that affects you, and your opinions taken into account.

Talking of a child separated from parents, the convention gives details of how, if separated, s/he must be taken care of by an authority or guardian. Also, if he is a refugee or has a disability and so on, s/he has some extra rights.

Article 24: Focuses on all aspects of good health of the child.

Article 28-29: Speaks of right to education—that too, it should help the child's personality and talents.

You Should Try to Understand Your Child

The child is a person in his own right. Parents need to understand it. The child's age and level of development determines how he understands the demands of an adult. If the parents do not know what is to be expected at each stage of development, they are likely to make too much, too little and unnecessary demands on the child.

Most parents tend to deal with the child either as a baby or as an adult and never as a person at a particular stage of development.

Take for example, a child of five or at times even ten years, the mother feeds him, bathes, washes his face, brushes his teeth, combs his hair, dresses him up, puts on his shoes and ties his shoe laces for him and packs his school bag for him. He is not a baby and can do all these tasks himself. In addition, it enables him to acquire age-appropriate skills.

Another example in contrast, is a child of three who is expected to read/write alphabets and numbers, do homework for long hours and should not play and waste time! This is a developmentally inappropriate demand.

All that he needs is to play. Here the child is expected to be grown up and responsible. The mother expects him to take responsibility and enjoy it. Depriving a child from play and make him do needless tasks for hours together is a crime against a child. In both the above cases, the mother feels stressed and frustrated when the child does not really understand what she wants him to do. Sometimes the child may resent it and rebel against her. When the child is comfortable – there is no friction between the child and the other/mother/teacher/caretaker.

What the child is capable of – he should do it himself. What he is not capable of – he should not be forced to do it. This can be determined not by the mother but by actually observing the child and doing only what is appropriate at that age.

Give Me Some Space

Aashrit is a five-and-a-half-years-old boy. His parents are in the software field and his brother is not yet admitted to any school or play-home. He was living with his parents and a younger brother, till his father got a job in the UK and moved there. Mother joined father with the younger child, entrusting Aashrit to the care of his paternal grandparents to continue his schooling (UKG). His grandparents were not in good health and they had their own life style between visiting temples and viewing television shows.

On a regular basis the grandparents received complaints from the school about the child. The complaints were – he doesn't read, write, draw, narrate stories and sing the rhymes. The child does all these activities at home according to the parents and grandparents but not in school. Such complaints prevailed even when his parents were in India.

The child looked very bored all the time. He was obese. He had restricted movements too. He was advised to get tested for thyroid. At this point, a lady from the neighbourhood met the child and offered to take him for a walk with her to Lalbagh. The grandparents knew him to be very reluctant to walk. But to their surprise, the child readily accepted the offer. Each step of his walk he enjoyed. In fact, he was reluctant to return home. It was not just on the school-going days, the same reluctance was exhibited on weekends also. He began enjoying looking at the bee-hives, different kinds of trees, flowers, birds, boards and maps. Aashrit, who was talking like an adult, began asking questions, expressing curiosity.

The next step was to carry a book to Lalbagh. Within two weeks of their walking together, the child wanted to get more books and he had learnt to read almost all the books they took, during their walks.

Gradually, he was introduced to the library close by. Initially, he was just handling the books in a cursory manner. Later on, he developed some interest in them and began looking into each book. He began to read the borrowed books to his grandparents. He began enjoying his class work and home work. All works were completed without anyone instructing him. He began getting 'stars' from the school for his performance. He enjoyed getting his stars by sharing them with his grandparents.

—Contributed by Rajalaksmi

The Child Should be Able to Understand You

Most parents love their children as a rule. Though there may be exceptions. But how many parents tell the child 'I love you'? How many of them hug the child and show affection through words or actions? If you don't, how will the child know that he is loved by you?

When you punish the child physically or verbally, he is likely to think he is unloved. A parent needs to learn that a child needs both affection and limit setting/discipline – but it should be understood by the child. So how does one show it? Verbally express what is there and what is expected of him/her. 'I love you but your screaming or fighting with your sister is not good. I don't approve of it. Say sorry and don't do it again.'

Children respect the parents who follow the 'just' rules and limit setting. But punishment should be used very little or not at all. If it is to be given, it should be discussed before hand with the child. Example: If you hit your sister, or have a temper tantrum, you will be given a 'time out' (optimum time, one minute per one-year age – 4-year-old gets four minutes). The idea is not to pay attention to bad behaviour but to encourage good behaviour. When the child plays with others, is helpful, takes care of self, rewards should be given. The reward must be something small and what the child likes.

A large number of parents believe that it is within their rights to punish the child. It is not a good idea. Praise and encouragement work better.

Behaviour of Parents

Children are keen observers of behaviour of adults. Often, they imitate the behaviour they see. A parent who is verbally or physically aggressive, very anxious and high strung often leads to imitative behaviour in children. When a child shows any kind of disturbed behaviour, ask yourself who else in the house or outside does it? Is it from the television? Is it from the teachers?

Parents must observe themselves, their behaviour their talk, interaction with others. Deception, cheating, lying, bragging are some such behaviours which children pick up from adults. They also pick up fearfulness and anxiety from parents.

If parents and family members constantly complain of pains and aches of the body or body parts, or tiredness or boredom, children take clues from that as well.

Parents should try to recognise their own behaviours and emotions in children. Once you recognise, the effort should be to eliminate it. Once you do that, the child's behaviour will automatically improve.

Parents, being moody, may have different rules at different times. This inconsistency may lead to confusion in the child.

Parents' Talk

Nagging all the time to make the child comply with instructions or saying 'No' all the time. If the child is a quiet child, constantly asking questions may not help, in fact, may make him unhappy and even more stubbornly refuse to comply. When a child is exuberant and talkative, you may find it annoying and may ask him to shut up. Then the child feels humiliated and may feel you do not care about him.

Children also learn the way to speak from you. Please talk in a polite manner even to a young child.

To Over-indulge or Deprive

Giving into all the demands of the child – does not help the child. He grows up believing that it is his right to get everything he asks. Such a child grows up to be selfish, self-centered and learns to make use of people.

Most times, genuine demands should be met, if it is not harmful, too expensive and cause trouble to others. By being neither overindulgent nor depriving, you make the child live in a happier world as s/he grows up.

Caring about Others (Pro-social Behaviour)

Always encourage children to think and feel how others think and feel. This is called *empathy*. While playing, sharing, being friendly, being helpful, considerate, praising others, caring about them should spontaneously occur to children. These need to be demonstrated by our own behaviour.

Negative Parenting

Parents routinely compare one child to another, be it at home, family or school. Being compared to another child about school performance, looks, behaviour, other achievements and talents, make the child inferior and jealous. All children are equal and no unfavourable comparison should be made. Instead of making them strive to achieve similar behaviour, it makes them angry against the child with whom they are compared.

Anger is Negative Emotion

It leads to poor interactions with children as it does with adults. Adults can fight back. Children, especially young children, cannot. Most children cannot handle anger of parents. Eventually, some of the children will be forced to retaliate in different ways.

Good Child

Vishala is a 10-year-old girl who was brought in for counselling as she had low academic performance and for being less active for the last one year. Both her parents are professional artistes. She is the only child and stays with her mother.

The mother of the child said that she and her husband were not in good terms and have decided to go for divorce. They both got into frequent arguments and often fought in front of Vishala and sometimes they came to blows.

According to the mother, Vishala is very mature, understanding and cooperative. She has been very easy to manage since birth and is like a friend to her. She consoles her mother whenever the parents fight. Though Vishala has been the witness of these arguments and fights, the mother has never spoken to her about separation. The child has learnt about it only by overhearing her mother talking to somebody. And she has told the mother, 'If you find it difficult to stay with daddy, leave him. I will be with you, let's stay in a different house'.

Vishala was asked to draw her family as she liked drawing. She made a drawing of a big family with all the extended family members. When she was asked to talk about her drawing, she said she wanted ALL her family members to stay together. She is a bright child, understanding and cooperative and has good emotional control. She is not very expressive and she feels she is the only support to her mother. She likes her father and wants to be with him, like her friends and cousins.

It was observed that Vishala's mother was not clear about separation and was even confused. The mother was counselled and encouraged to discuss with her family and/or friends about separation. She was also advised to go for marital counselling if needed. The importance of communication was explained to the mother and she was encouraged to talk directly to the child about the things happening in the family. (She felt there was no need to talk as Vishala was stronger than the mother).

It was clear that Vishala is interested in singing, dancing, painting and drawing. It was suggested to the mother that the child spend time regularly on these activities. The mother felt that she needed to discuss about separation with her family and eventually did so.

She also felt they needed to take professional help as they never thought of ways to solve their problems. They met a counsellor and decided to give some more time to each other. The mother spoke to Vishala about all these in detail and asked what she felt about it. Vishala, for the very first time, told her mother what and how she felt and broke down. The child told the mother that she is happy that the mother spoke to her.

Vishala and her mother have decided to speak to each other about their thoughts and feelings. The mother feels that Vishala is becoming like earlier, active and cheerful.

—Contributed by Sindhu Karanth

Partiality in Treating Children and Adults

For whatever reason, because someone has higher social status or superiority of some kind, you may give him a special status. Or someone is weak and old, you may treat them with disdain and neglect. For example, the father and boys get the first preference for food, good clothes etc. A girl is a second-class citizen. Sometimes these are expressed through talk. 'You are a girl, you don't need it' or you send the boy to private school and the girl to government school. One needs to learn to be impartial.

Son, an Uncrowned Prince

Sunil, the youngest of three children, was brought for counselling for difficult behaviour along with his second elder sister, Shwetha who came with complaints of lack of concentration in studies and decreasing grades.

Sunil had lots of demands and did not obey parents and his sisters. Sunil had even stolen some money once, which triggered the family to come for counselling. In the course of counselling, it became apparent that the reason for both children's problems were surprisingly the same and unknowingly, it was the parents who were creating the problem.

The parents had only one son, that too, after two daughters. He was the prince of the family. All his demands were met unconditionally. Daughters were told that since he is a small boy, his demands had to be taken care of. The father never talked to the daughters and he was not able to connect to them emotionally. This created a lot of emotional problems in Shwetha, resulting in lowered grades. Sunil, being always told 'yes', was never ready to take a 'no' for answer, which resulted in his conduct problem.

The parents were encouraging the son while neglecting the daughters. According to parents, they were meeting all of Sunil's demands, not because he was a son but because he was the youngest.

But Shwetha had a completely different story to tell. According to her, since he was a boy, his demands were met and since she was a girl, her demands were not even heard. Also, since the father failed to connect emotionally to the daughters, they felt completely neglected.

Mother was actually a step-mother to the daughters. Their own mother had died few days after Shwetha's birth and the father had married his wife's sister. The children did not know this. They thought that she was their mother. She treated them well like their own mother would have. Even the step-mother admitted that her husband did not talk to the daughters and she felt helpless as she did not know how to help them connect.

This is an example of what happens when one child is given more importance in front of other child/children and when there is poor communication between family members.

—Contributed by Mithila Sharma

Parental Ambitions

All of us want our children to be high achievers. And we believe that children should achieve our ambitions. He or she should be an IT professional, doctor, scientist and so on. But the child may not have the same ambitions. Also, children have different ambitions at different stages of development. So, they fail to appreciate our ambitions.

- A small child may want to be bus conductor or vegetable vendor.
- An older child may want to be a cricketer or a film star.

- When reaching adolescence, they discover for themselves what they would like to be.

Their interest may not match with parental ambitions. But remember that the child's ambitions should chart the course of his life.

Making the Child Guilty

When you fail to make the child follow your ambitions, you adopt dangerous method of making them feel guilty. You make them guilty by saying, 'I have taken care of you, worked so hard to give all the comfort and education. Is it the way you repay me?' Constantly reminding the child about your sacrifices makes your children guilt prone. Why do young students commit suicide when they fail in the examinations? In fact, *examinations are the least important aspect of one's education, in its real sense.*

Parents must not make children so guilty that they start believing that life is not worth living – if the child does not fulfil the ambitions of parents. The question is whether you want a happy child or unhappy, and at times, even a dead one?

The Final Advice

Let your children play and be happy.

Can you smile like me?

3

The Cycle of Growing Up Woman and Child

INCLUSION OF women in a book on children may appear strange. Both ancient indigenous health systems of India and the current research in developmental psychology point in the same direction, especially in early childhood—of mother-child interaction. Both deduce this is of utmost importance. Mother-Child bonding and attachment plays a significant role in promoting or warping the overall development of the child.

Some of the major current trends in psychology are: developmental psychology, health, psychology, positive psychology and evolutionary psychology. **Developmental psychology** postulates that bio-psycho-social contexts are the basis of development as one moves across the developmental phases from conception to death. **Health psychology** highlights the importance of bio-psycho-social determinants in their interactions with environmental factors and their effects on initiating, maintaining and healing physical and psychological diseases. **Positive psychology** de emphasises the disease model and focuses on positive experience. **Evolutionary psychology** focuses on animal models and draws parallel with human development. All the above trends have relevance to how we deal with the various stages of development, especially of children and women.

Developmental approach or life cycle approach is of immense relevance to study women and children.

Bio-psycho-social contexts are crucial for development, be at normal or otherwise. The understanding of continuities or discontinuities is important. Critical stages in development too receive attention. Thus, there are critical stages in the learning process through infancy to childhood as well as emotional and social development of women with definite impact of pregnancy and birth of a child. These are examples of some critical phases of development:

- Interaction between the infant and the mother leading to bonding and secure attachment.
- Interaction between child and the peers leading to first step towards socialisation.
- Interaction between child and the teacher, leading to learning.
- Interaction between adolescent and peers leading to growth and ego identity.
- Youth-career and occupational stability.
- Youth and marriage.
- Once again, the cycle of child and the parent status.
- When the children grow and launch out, the 'empty nest syndrome' is faced by middle-aged parents.
- Old-age-health, boredom and loneliness, alienation from children.

Developmental psychologists have gained much knowledge from the studies on infants and children. These studies offer stark contrast to notions held earlier such as 'mind is a clean slate' at birth and a newborn's mind being 'blooming buzzing confusion'.

A child is born with cognitive skills, being prepared for acquisition of language and innate emotional disposition or temperament. Four stages of Piagetian cognitive development trace the development of logic in childhood using the processes of assimilation and accommodation. Darwin's theory of evolution, works of Jean Piaget, Chomsky, temperament research point in the same direction. Empirical studies in childhood by developmental psychologists disprove the common belief of adults that they need to teach children. *Children inherently have a great potential for learning.*

In order to prove that children have the inborn skills to learn and adults only need to facilitate learning, the author conducted a series of studies with 2000 rural and tribal children. The studies revealed that only through free play, their functional skills of attention, language, intelligence, creativity, memory and number work significantly improved over twenty play sessions, with one-and-a-half hours each day. This leads us to the insight that the gap that exists between education and child development can be bridged through play.

In ancient times in India, in the sole Ayurvedic paediatric treatise *Kashyapa Samhita* there is clear description of foetal development along with description of how the foetus feels pain and pleasure, how the intelligence dawns and so on. These notions are currently being empirically supported. Even the *Samskaras* of childhood suggests the clear evidence of understanding of developmental phases.

Child development research highlights the fact that all the domains of development in the physical, intellectual, language, cognitive, emotional, social, sexual and moral domain occurs through play.

In the modern Indian scenario, however, academic achievement rules the roost at the cost of play. The parents see academic success as the only goal whereas only a happy child should be in the focus.

Life cycle approach and women has crucial aspects as follows:

- Individual life cycle and development.
- Familial life cycles at home – Indian family systems of greater complexity, involving honour, respect, loyalty as well as unexpressed hostility, depression and so on.
- Social life cycle – the roles to be played at different stages in life of a woman at HOME and WORK PLACE. The balancing of home and work, child care, professional ambition comes along with joy, conflicts and frustration. Achieving a balance among the above requires new skills to be learnt. Mother-child interaction does not remain the same. *It constantly has to evolve—when to provide close physical and emotional warmth to a young infant, when to allow them to separate from the mother and socialise with other children, and when to let them go and grow to be adults are very important issues to understand.*

Who is More Vulnerable? Women or Men?

Research in the area of mental health shows that if one adopts developmental approach certain interesting findings emerge:

Girls are biologically less vulnerable to physical illness, abortion, infant mortality and fatal illnesses.

In the prevalence of psychological disorders, boys have a higher prevalence than girls.

At adolescence, the ratios of disorders even out and thereafter, women have more psychological problems than men. *The reasons possibly could be bio-psycho-social parameters which differ between the genders in their life time trajectories.*

Understanding of Experiences

Children and women need to be developmental in perspective, otherwise the rich texture of understanding will be faulty and misleading. Simply importing Western experiences and tests is not a productive effort. *One has to understand one's own culture and follow the developmental factors using experiential methods.* This would yield rich dividends.

How can we understand our own lives if we do not pay attention to the culture we come from?

Tiger Moms (An Asian Model)

Highly ambitious mother (parent) makes the children excel in studies/art/music by constantly pressurising them. The children do grow up to be high achievers, yet unhappy persons. One of the famous tiger mom's children wrote about how miserable they were. A variant of tiger parenting is the 'helicopter' parenting where children are constantly supervised.

Always First!

Eight-year-old Preeti is a happy bright girl who likes to dress up and look pretty. She is friendly and good at studies. Preeti and her parents came for counselling for four months. Her father was a businessman and mother a home maker. Both the parents are college educated. Her mother was extremely worried about Preeti's decline in academic performance and her rude behaviour.

During the counselling, what caused so much distress and worry in her mother was revealed. Preeti was caught by her teachers when she pushed her classmates to reach the playground 'first' when the bell rang for the PT period. She copied all the answers at the math test from the neighbour so she would get all the answers correct, rather than rely on her knowledge to solve the problems. She was often very rude to her mother and lied about little things. She liked to wear makeup like an adult, for which there was often fights with her mother.

A clearer picture of the situation emerged over the sessions. Preeti and her parents lived with her grandparents, along with the families of her paternal uncles, until two years ago. She was the youngest in the family, where she was showered lots of attention. Her mom used to help her with the homework and made sure Preeti was always first in class. She was told that even if she did not understand anything in the class, her mom would be there to teach her everything.

When both the paternal grandparents died, the brothers split and moved into their own houses. Around the same time, when Preeti was 7, her baby brother was born and she went to her maternal grandparents' house with her mother for a couple of months. With her mother busy with the new baby, Preeti spent more time with her mother's younger sister who was working. She dressed to go to work every day, looking pretty. Preeti also saw that the aunt was a lot 'cooler' than her own mom or grandmother. She did not hesitate to let everyone know her opinion and was very expressive and vocal.

When Preeti returned home with her mother and younger brother, she did not have any friends to play with. Her mother was often busy with the baby and Preeti was expected to take care of her studies, books and learn well at school and come first in her class. When her mother asked Preeti to finish her homework and get ready to go to school, she would lie that she had done it already. Later, the parents got to know that she copied during tests and would not allow anyone to go out of the class first when the bell rang.

Her grades had dropped and whenever her mother talked to Preeti, she would be rude and answer back.

The young bright child who had cousins and friends to play with had to move away where she did not have friends. Because they lived on a main road with heavy traffic, she had to stay indoors. She could not play with kids her age. During her free time, she started to dress up like her aunt and talk like her. Her mother could not give her enough time to teach or play as she was busy with the baby. Preeti had to keep up with her first position and she started to copy and lie as she did not know any other way to keep her first position.

Preeti's mother was made to understand that she needed to help her child enjoy learning rather than focus on the rat race of getting first rank. Preeti needed to spend at least half to one hour playing in the park with kids her age. She was asked to focus on Preeti's positive behaviour and gently get her into a routine of reading her lessons and learn new things, rather than focus on getting first rank. The mother was asked to make changes in her routine, so she would get to spend some quality time with Preeti. Over time the situation improved.

—Contributed by Anitha Sudheer

Some illustrations of Indian indigenous experiences highlight the need to examine and adopt some preferred practices based on ancient wisdom.

One among them is **Infant-Mother bonding**. The bonding occurs not only after the birth but even before the birth.

In Ayurveda, the pregnant woman is given many a sound advice about physical and psychological wellbeing as her ill-health and distress can adversely affect the foetus. The social rituals provide much-needed support to the expectant mother. There are several rituals related to pregnancy which are observed in traditional families even today. For example, around the seventh month of pregnancy after ritual celebration, the pregnant woman is taken care of in her maternal home. Even after the birth of the infant she stays with her mother for a prolonged period, gradually learning how to feed, bathe and take care of the baby. Special meals, massages and oil baths enable the young mother to go to her marital home and take care of the baby herself. Oil bath and massages are very preferred practices in childcare.

The importance of total support for the women during pregnancy and child birth, till the child can be managed is an extraordinarily well thought out social ritual. This is the phase in life when women are most vulnerable to physical and psychosocial stressors.

Similar rituals,which are called *Samskara*s, are provided for the child during the developmental stages such as naming, tonsure, first feeding of cereals, ear piercing and so on. The important ritual of 'upanayana' between 7 to 11 years indicates the readiness of the child to acquire scholastic skills.

Our traditions say, a child has the physical and psychological maturity to learn at the age of 7 years, obviously forcing him to learn scholastic skills before that is a very unhealthy practice. However, this is widely practised in India and the Asian countries.

The life cycle approach promotes the view that the mother needs to hold the baby very close when very young, but let them go free when they are ready to relate to other children and eventually adults too. The important part to note, the mother has to adopt different roles at different stages of her own life and the various stages in the child's own life. But most people get fixed at one stage, disregarding the fact that all of us are going through different stages of life. One cannot simply use the same method all the time.

Traditional Baby Bath

Art by Kshama Rau

Steps in Baby Bath

In the picture the baby is lying on his abdomen with head raised in the direction of mother's feet. An infant who is younger than six months, he is laid on his back on his mother's lap with his head raised towards mother's lap. If the baby is place on the ground on a plastic sheet, the baby may swallow water. In this prone position resting between mother's legs, the water that is poured drains away safely. While washing the head, mother's palms shelters the head and protects the baby's face, especially eyes, nose and mouth. The baby is thoroughly massaged, mildly exercised and given warm bath. Then gently dried with soft cloth and often dried under incense smoke. After this, the baby is fed and made to go to sleep.[2]

Advantages

- Touching and massaging enhance tactile and kinaesthetic functioning (touch and movements).
- Holding the baby so that it touches the mother's body enhances emotional bonding.
- Massage for infants promotes overall development and not just physical development.
- In the contemporary paediatric practice, massage is used as an intervention for high risk.

Some Examples

- The child wants to feed himself. Mother will persist in feeding him – in fact, leading to fussy eating all his life.
- The child of 3 years continuously asks questions – Why this? Why that? The mother finds it annoying – she shuts him up by saying,'Don't bother me'. The mother does not know how important this is in the development of language, intelligence, positive social interactions for the child.
- Later on, when he goes to school, college and so on, she expects him to talk a lot and take interest in her because she is his mother. But why would he feel that he should talk to her?
- When he is an adolescent and mature, he knows his mind and has strong bonding with his friends, he may not share anything with the mother.

---

[2] It is to be noted that the water used for bathing should be luke warm and never hot. In South India very hot water is used for washing the head. It is known to produce epileptic fits and could induce seizure. Prevention is using luke warm water or sponge wash and reducing the fever before it goes high. In the event of fits, always consult paediatric neurologist as repeated fits cause damage to the brain.

There is an old saying,'Pamper up to 5 years, punish for 10 years and treat your son as a friend from his 16th year'. It is interesting that the word *shiksha* refers both to teaching and punishment.

Indian life cycle approach holds that in our behaviour and speech at the right time, the right place and the right person is crucial to health and wellbeing of an individual.

4

Children and Violence

THIS CHAPTER deals with the subject of children and violence in two sections. In the first section the focus is on visual media and violence. In the second section, violence and children in general and in Indian society in particular.

Visual Media & Violence

In the modern era, films for children have been the earliest-format visual media for children.

Films play the role of the most potent instrument of transmission of culture to children, intentional or not, beneficial or not. Films have an unavoidable and arresting presence, reflecting and shaping social identities and behaviours. However, films need to be developmentally appropriate–that is to the level of understanding at the cognitive, language, emotional, social and moral levels of the child at each phase of the child's development. So, the themes, languages, constructs and actions might be understood by the child differently when she/he is two or three, five or six or seven or ten years old.

In the 20th century, when dealing with films, the parents/ children had to go and see the movies in a picture hall.

A major transition occurred with the advent of the television—when films became accessible at home. The present focus is on visual media such as cinema, television, video, cable and satellite television along with computer games and the mobile and their effects on children. The beneficial effects in terms of education undoubtedly are there, but that is not the point of discussion here.

Since the advent of the technology of television, there have been a number of studies measuring the impact of television viewing in the laboratory and field settings of short term and longitudinal nature. Some interesting examples from the USA, Canada and South Africa provide the following data to be used as a backdrop to the argument that is being put forth.

What is the effect of television on the entire population?

Centerwall studied the homicide rates in the whole White population in USA and Canada before 1974, and in South Africa where television was introduced after 1975.

In the USA between 1945 and 1974 homicide rates rose from 3.00 to 5.8 per 100,000 (an increase of 93%) and in Canada from 1.3 to 2.5 per 100,000 showing a 92 per cent increase while in South Africa in the same period there was decrease of 7 per cent from 2.7 to 2.5 per 100,000.

In South Africa between 1973 and 1983, after television was introduced, there was a 56 per cent increase and of 130 per cent in 1987. In contrast, in the USA and Canada there has been no further increase since 1974, suggesting that there has been a saturation point.

What relevance does the data have for effects on children?

On further analysis, Centerwall reported that there was a lag time of 10-15 years between the introduction of television and doubling of homicide rates. Serious violence appeared to have first begun with children, then adolescents and young youth in the first generation of television viewers. This has important implications for those concerned with media effects on children.

Early reports on children and relationship consequent to physical and verbal aggression came from Joy et al in a study of a small Canadian town which they called 'Notel' before and after the introduction of the television and two control towns who already had television. A cohort of 45 first and second graders was observed prospectively, for 2 years on objectively measured acts of physical aggression such as hitting, biting etc. Rates did not change in the control groups, but in Notel, it increased by 160 per cent.

Eron and Huesmann followed up a cohort of 875 children in a semi-rural US county and reported that television viewing at 8 years predicted serious acts of crime by the age of 30, particularly in boys (the Columbia Cohort study).

In a retrospective control study, Kruttschniff et al compared 100 male felons and 65 men without history of offence. They matched them on age, race, track of residence, and after controlling for school performance, exposure to parental violence and baseline criminality, and childhood exposure to television violence, the study found that the scores approached statistical significance. Most of the Canadian and US studies of effect of prolonged childhood exposure to television (2 years or more) show positive relationship, contributing a later physical aggression, though all of them do not reach statistically significant level.

A South African study by Conradie et a1 of 10,000 White children of whom and 2,200 followed up for 5 years, 2 years before and 3 years after the introduction of television, reported significant increase in physical and verbal aggression. The study suggested that it was a cumulative process.

These studies appear to suggest: viewing of violence on screen by children has adverse effect in terms of facilitating subsequent aggressive behaviour.

However, those in the industry of media ask an ingenious question. Would you become a serial murderer after seeing a movie on the theme? Some suggest even a 'cathartic' value—that it relieves aggression without the person acting upon it. There are other more important contributors such as poverty, family violence as well. Thus, a definite suggestion predisposing personality traits and vulnerability, make some children more vulnerable than most. This controversy reflects a basic difference in the bias towards environmental or genetic contributors.

One may view it from different vantage points:

a. *Television contributing factor to violence*

Only the vulnerable children along with non-supportive families and low socio-economic status and who extensively view television violence are likely to end up as criminals, while for the majority it is an innocuous or even an educative medium.

However, the research trends have changed a good deal in the recent year. The US Commission on Causes and Prevention of Violence in 1969 had stated that television was *not principal cause but a contributing factor* along with low income, unstable homes, while the 1982 update has supported a closer positive relationship.

b. *Aggression is a learnt behaviour*

Longitudinal studies by Milavsky et al suggested a small effect, along with other predictors as environment on personality. The British and Finnish studies tend to support more environmental vantage point. Experimental studies showed that violence is learnt through different ways through the visual media:

i. Imitation
ii. Activating latent tendencies for aggression
iii. Desensitisation to sympathy for the victim. If one is perpetually exposed to violence, one becomes insensitive to it.
iv. Accept violence as normal way to conflict resolution There have been a spate of reports of young offenders and special is the sensational case of torture and murder of two-year-old James Bugler by two ten-year-old boys in UK, where television/video were seen as major contributors as these children did not come from disturbed families.

British television-related violence and crime rates among adolescents are less than US television-related violence and crime rates. Many of the retrospective studies suggest stronger links than earlier suspected. Eron and Huesmann linked violent crime, wife and child abuse across all socioeconomic strata and IQ. Bailey reported that viewing of violent and pornographic videos was a significant casual factor for subsequent act.

The study by UNESCO in 1996-97, the largest study spanning twenty-three nations of 5,000 twelve-year-old pupils revealed wide accessibility—more than three hours a day of television viewing—next only to school hours. This study found that children turn to violence to solve problems.[3]

In 2001, the Centre for Advocacy and Research (CFAR) studied the impact of media violence on children in five Indian

[3] Net-accessed material.

cities of Delhi, Lucknow, Calcutta, Hyderabad and Ahmedabad with children between 6 to 12-year-old. Their study reported high and consistence level of violence on television in all forms of programmes.

Thus, most international and Indian studies mostly agree on the presence of violence on television and agree that they influence children.

c. *Understanding aggression*

In a dynamic approach to understanding of aggression, Centerwall highlighted the role of television in the development of superego, replacing the family which was the sole influencing agent before the advent of television. He even claimed that if television technology had not been there, there would have been 10,000 less homicides, 70,000 less rapes and 70,000 less of other minor crimes each year in the USA.

d. *Understanding is stage-specific*

Developmental psychologists have highlighted stages of moral development where between the age of 1 and 4 years there is self-centered morality. At 5 years there is more acceptability of morality and between 5 and 7 years preoccupation with justice. It is between 8-14 years that children are concerned that people should think well of them.

Thus, what the child views and understands depends on his/her stage of development. What it means to the programmer may be understood quite differently by the child at different stages of development. The same content may be understood differently by children in different developmental stages.

e. *Context of entertainment as projected by the industry*

i. A notion that it is all fun and a way to while away time.
ii. Child receives distorted images which he/she has not experienced. This is especially dangerous when love, sex and violence are equated.

iii. Brutality is portrayed to escalate the appeal to the jaded.
iv. Victims are portrayed as sub-human and thus, are not to be pitied.
v. Victims deserve violent treatment.

(For example, Robert and John who murdered little Jaime explained that the baby had to be hit 30 times because he kept getting up. While explaining, these older children did not even realise how much pain they were causing to this little child!)

The industry spends billions on advertising as they know about the impact of the visual media. The protagonists of uncensored programmes fail to recognise the differing levels and stages of maturity and stability. They do not know the level of imagination children are capable of, and how they can desensitise a child by using the flooding techniques by systematic repetition, thus reducing the original accompanying emotion.

I take the position that indiscriminate viewing of visual media, especially with violent content, interferes with normal development as seen from my own field and clinical experience, psychodynamic and behavioural theories and most of all from a developmental perspective.

A child attains normal development in the different domains such as physical, cognitive, language, emotional, social, moral and sexual development. These occur in specific unique fashion, in infancy, childhood (early, middle and late) and adolescence (early and late). Any event is seen, understood and responded to differently by children at the different stages of its growth.

Most of the programmes are created by adults who presume to know the developmental levels of the children.

The child goes through four stages of cognitive development and can understand the events limited by understanding of that particular stage. It is thus essential that a child is explained about the meaning of the event as meant to be conveyed. A child may completely misunderstand the message.

My own experience with children brought to a child guidance centre reveals the impact of indiscriminate television viewing.

Our experience in the Indian context show, regardless of the age of the child, television viewing indiscriminately has serious repercussions. These may manifest as poor interaction with the caretakers. A four-month-old baby exposed continuously to a television screen reacts to violent scenes with fear. Long-term social and emotional deprivation coupled with long hours of television viewing has been encountered in children present with Autistic symptoms. Short-term manifestation of aggression, whining, temper tantrums and fear reaction soon after hours of television viewing too has been noted.

In an interesting experience of 800 tribal primary school children who were not exposed to television at all as they had no electricity connection where they lived, complete absence of aggression, hyperactivity and attention deficit was noted in a study I had conducted.

The Indian Scenario

1. Adults and children share television viewing and very few of them are suitable for young children.
2. Adults and children alike view television into late hours, thus depriving children of much-needed sleep and long exposure to television.
3. Anecdotal accounts of reduced interest in school work both in cities and rural areas.
4. Especially since the advent of video, cable and satellite techniques, there is unlimited supply of unsuitable material in one's own home.

5. Use of television as baby sitters.
6. Viewing of television is encouraged instead of play. Play promotes the overall development of children.

This situation cannot be allowed to continue. But what are the problems in countering this practice? Newson has aptly stated that even liberated generations have been naive in permitting the present practices to go unquestioned.

Following are some of the suggestions:

1. For strict control of programmes (unacceptable to the industry and biological protagonists who believe that its heredity that matters and not the environment).
2. As the effect on children is particularly devastating, the intervention should be aimed at **parental control** of television viewing and **promotion of positive moral values in the home environment.**
3. The content of the programmes should **provide healthy role models** with **prosocial behaviour.**
4. Promote suitable programmes to different age groups.
5. Awareness campaign to public on ill effects and hope for self-denial by the corporate sector which control the media industry.
6. **Encouragement to play** instead of television viewing to promote healthy overall development.

In conclusion, there are many factors contributing to violence among children. These could be domestic, violence in schools and violence in the community emerging out of individual and social causes. These also in turn create a cycle of violence among and against children. However, there are child policies and laws in place to counter the above to the extent possible. There are organisations working towards the amelioration of family and social pathologies. But there is nothing in place to protect our children from the ubiquitous visual media.

Though international and Indian studies mostly agree on the presence of violence in the visual media and blame the media for its negative impact on children – these findings have mostly been ignored. The reasons may be:

i. Because it is obvious that rising violence cannot be attributed to only the visual media. There are other potent causes of violence as domestic violence, war, riots, impact of natural disaster which exposes the children directly to violence.
ii. Because correlation does not mean causation. Increased media portrayal of violence and violence among children and adolescent does not mean that one is caused by the other.
iii. The studies should unequivocally prove the cause and effect of violence. The studies thus need to be methodologically sound and fine-grained analysis, using cross sectional and longitudinal methodologies.
iv. Most importantly the effects should be studied in the developmental context, through infancy, childhood and adolescence – as the impact is likely to be very different in the developmental trajectory at different ages.
v. The studies also should emphasise on intervention strategies at media, community and home spheres.

Violence against Children

Violence needs to be viewed from a much broader perspective as violence against children cannot be examined in any other context. There is a need to examine the following aspects:

1. Violence perpetrated intentionally or not.

2. Violence that is manifest (serious) or latent or less obvious, nevertheless serious in its impact.
3. At home, schools and even in institutions that are supposed to be safe havens for them such as orphanages, refugee camps and remand homes.
4. Even when the population or a particular community as a whole is exposed to deliberate violence as in wars or riots, children are particularly vulnerable when adults become helpless in providing physical or emotional succour that they deserve.
5. In natural or man-made disasters children may suffer because of the impact of the events on their caretakers due to deprivations of different sorts against children.
6. Violence against children can have negative impact on their physical or psychological health.
7. Response to violence witnessed or experienced is determined by the developmental stage of the child and his temperament.
8. Violence may be elicited by factors like race, ethnicity, gender or even psychological and physical disabilities, making them more vulnerable.
9. Violence against children or exposure to it may result in violence by the children themselves.

Some Definitions of Physical and Emotional Maltreatment

- **Legal:** Harm actual or likely: physical, sexual and non-physical, emotional, impairment of health (including mental health), developmental domains such as physical, intellectual, emotional, social or behavioural development.
- **Medical:** Physical evidence and proof of emotional abuse such as neglect, deprived attention, rejection, social

isolation, threat of abandonment, age inappropriate demands as imposed by child labour.

- **Cultural:** Perspectives vary as to what constitute physical or psychological abuse across cultures.
- Child outcome thus should be the key criterion.
- Short term and long-term outcomes with or without intervention.
- The abuse is intentional or not, it still hurts.

Thus, deliberate or otherwise, violence can have short term or long term adverse impact on the physical and/or mental health of children. Some of the psychological explanatory theories are:

- Learning theories
- Psychodynamic theories
- Developmental psychology
- Clinical experience: some case illustrations and field studies

In the following section an attempt is made to examine some of the above aspects.

Unintended Violence at Home

Effect of maternal psychiatric disorders on children:

Infants and children are entirely dependent on mother for nurturance, physical and psychological survival. The pathways from parental illness lead to effects on children.

1. Infanticide, injury, failure to thrive and other forms of abuse.
2. Indirect effects because of psychiatric consequence of mental illness on the marital partner.
3. Marital disharmony as a consequence of mental illness in one parent.
4. Impairment of mother's interaction with the child.

5. Temporary or permanent separation as a consequence of the mother's illness.
6. Exposure to violence through movies, videos, video games and variants of virtual reality.

Home and School Stressors

Sumana is a 14-year-old girl in 7th standard. When she was around 6 years old, she lost her father who was very abusive. Her mother did odd jobs as construction worker/domestic help or store worker and took care of her only child Sumana. Later Sumana was put into a residential school from 4th standard. When she was in 5th standard, her mother passed away due to some illness. Sumana does not know the proper details of her mother's illness and death. Till she completed 6th standard, there was confusion about who has to take care of her. Later, her maternal uncles decided to take care of her and called her back from the hostel. From then on, she stays in a joint family of her uncles and attends a regular school. In school, the teachers complained that Sumana was aggressive, quarrelsome, and stubborn and used abusive language ever since she joined. She showed little interest in academics and had behavioural problems.

It was observed that though the child appeared to be very talkative and disruptive, she did not express her thoughts and feelings. She had not been given any positive feedback since she had joined the new school and was receiving a lot of negative comments from her peers and teachers.

Initially, the counsellor greeted the child every day and spoke to her for few minutes. This helped greatly in quickly building rapport and winning her confidence. Through activities it was observed that she was good in sports and could read well, especially English. Hence, she was complimented on those aspects and encouraged to participate in more and more activities. Very soon she appeared more cheerful and confident.

Though she participated in activities like sports, games, story reading, singing and dancing, she refused to make drawings both individually and in groups. She was encouraged to draw every time and only once did she comply, making some drawing about her friends from the old school. She was appreciated for her drawing and made to speak about those friends. She opened up a little bit saying, she missed them a lot. She was given feedback that she is active, energetic and very helpful. This would help her win friends very easily. This appeared to boost her confidence and soon she made a few friends. She was given tasks like helping friends in group activities, teaching younger children to read. This made her relationships with peers stronger.

During story sessions, acceptable and non-acceptable behaviours were explained through stories and the child was made to discuss with peers about which behaviours to pick up and which ones not to.

The teachers were informed about her family background and requested to deal with her more positively. They were asked to appreciate every positive act of her's and talk to her gently. Subsequently, positive changes in her behaviour were observed by her teachers. She was more cheerful and friendly than earlier. She participated in more activities including academic activities.

—Contributed by Sindhu Karanth

Schizophrenia and manic-depressive disorder in the mother have been found in some studies in terms of less social contact with the children. Substance abuse by the mother places the children at greater risk directly by the maternal drug intake during pregnancy and indirectly by poor mothering. Parental marital discord, sibling and family discords contribute to risk. Chronic physical illnesses in the parents or in the child can place the child at higher risk for abuse can often have negative impact on children though the child is not directly subject to this violence.

Violence in the Community and its Impact on Children

A study from Ireland about the impact of violence on children found them also to be a part of social turmoil. The study suggested a process of habituation and noted that children's subjective realities fairly reflect the objective situation.

Impact of Physical Illness on Child and Family

Venu is a boy of 15 years who came with complaints of poor performance in academics and fear of being alone since age 3, and bed-wetting for the past one year before he sought help.

The child was diagnosed to be diabetic from the age of two-and-a-half years and he had developed epilepsy, for which he was under medication. He was also short sighted since the age of 8 years. He occasionally got muscle cramps.

The family of the child consisted of father, mother, one elder brother and one younger brother. The parents had consanguineous marriage (father was mother's maternal uncle).

The detailed history of the child showed developmental delays. He had poor vision when he was 6 ½ years. He could speak at 3 years of age. He had articulation problems during childhood and even now his speech was minimal. Physically, he had many problems like diabetes, epilepsy and short sightedness. The intelligence level of the child when tested was below average.

The mother was diagnosed with tuberculosis and treated for it when the child was 6 months old. The family history showed that the father was epileptic when he was young and he was also a diabetic.

The family had several psychological problems as well. The father was quarrelsome. He suspected that the mother has had extra marital affairs and also felt that the elder and younger sons were not his own as they were not diabetic and epileptic. The eldest son in the family had left studying even though he was studying well, as he was not able to bear the harassment by the father. The younger one stayed with the grandparents for the same reason and he came to see his mother once in a while. The father quarrelled with whoever talked in favour of the mother and accused her always of having affairs. There was not enough money for maintenance of the family also.

For all the above reasons, the child and the mother were depressed. The child, with many physical disabilities, was unable to cope up with the situation or was also not able to move away from it and thus had to face it. Venu was guided to take the vocational training programme so that he could have some livelihood skills and help himself.

—*Contributed by Arathi Rao*

Intended Violence: Sexual and Physical Abuse

These may occur at home or outside home. Some of the common examples in the Indian context are child labour, child prostitution and pornography. These are breeding ground for sexual and physical abuse.

There is growing evidence suggesting that sexual abuse is not only a fleeting trauma but may have long term disastrous consequences. Recovery from physical abuse, though immediately traumatic on the child and the family, is possible; sexual abuse may have long term effect on sexuality, emotional adjustment and intimate relationship. The issues are complex as these deal with family, legal and therapeutic issues.

O Father Save Me!

Netravati, a tribal girl, was studying in a junior college. She was from a poor family and stayed in a free hostel run for her community girls. She was good at studies. She was considered a joker in her hostel. She was jovial, lively and made everyone around her laugh.

The warden of the hostel was told secretly by some of the inmates that Netravati wept during nights. Warden's only proof for this report was that she too had witnessed her swollen eyes and red nose during mornings. When questioned, as always, Netravati made the warden laugh by making one of her unique and inimitable jokes. She never replied to any specific question.

After checking it herself for some days and getting no convincing reply from her, the warden thought of getting some professional help. She met the counsellor first and narrated her observations along with the other inmates'. Then she sent Netravati to attend a counselling session. The story that followed was an astounding one.

Netravati longed for her father, when she went to sleep—this was the first information she brought out. The story line goes somewhat like this: her mother re-married, leaving her first husband, when Netravati was 4 years old. From then on, till she was 12 years old, that is for 8 long years, continuously, she was the victim of sexual abuse by her step father. This was during day time, after her school and before her mother returned home from her daily work in the fields. It was stopped when her mother left him and moved away from him. The child never opened her mouth regarding this as she was threatened by him not to disclose anything to her mother. Even her mother was totally unaware or ignorant of this daily humiliation the child was subjected to for such a long period.

She was tortured by the burning feelings of shame and guilt. She longed for her father, to be with her to protect her from any vicious person. This longing expressed itself in the form of crying during nights, hidden from the whole world.

—Contributed by Rajalakshmi

Those who point out at the dress of women as the main and sometimes the sole tempting factor in any sexual abuse cases – would they suggest what dress a 4-year-old girl child should wear to save herself from her own father figure at home abusing her?

Gender Inequality

Among children, survival rates are better for boys than girls. This is true of childhood, adolescence and during the child-bearing age for the female.

A study of diet and nutritional status of the girl child by the National Institute of Nutrition indicated that though there was social preference for boys and they were given prolonged breastfeeding and taken more often to doctors, there was no deliberate discrimination against a girl child with reference to diet and nutrition.

However, other studies report significant discriminatory practices regarding nutrition, provision of medical care and education in favour of boys. Female infanticide and abortion are practised in certain pockets in the country, for example in Tamil Nadu, Haryana and Rajasthan. Nowadays abortion of female foetus after amniocentesis test in urban middle and upper-class groups is quite common. The surviving female child, thus, may not be deliberately discriminated against.

Better health care of females at all ages, with improved educational and economic status, would lead to improved health status of the children including the female children. Provision of mental health services to this group appears to be too vast a task to be dealt with, except for education of the community across the country as a whole.

It is noted that the provision of programmes for the betterment of children's health, welfare and education alone are not sufficient. It is important to create conditions which would permit the girl child to benefit from these programmes. *Female children above the age of six years to late adolescence are not sufficiently helped by the existing national and State programmes.* Gender bias, however, is not merely confined to the poor alone; affluent sections of the society also practise it.

Psychosocial Development of Children at Risk

Children from deprived socio-economic and educational background, such as street children, working children and institutionalised children, form a population at risk with reference to normal psychosocial development. They are more vulnerable to emotional disorders because of psychosocial stressors in the early and formative years of development.

Research across the world reveals that socio-economic and educational background of the parents influence child-rearing practices. This, in turn, affects the psychosocial development of the children. Psychosocial development consists of cognitive, language, emotional, social, sexual and moral development. In each of these areas, apart from the hereditary endowment of the child, emotionally congenial family and peer interactions and a cognitively stimulating environment are essential for healthy overall development.

Research has shown that deprived socio-economic and educational background can have a devastating effect on cognitive and language development. Studies on emotionally deprived children show that they have difficulties in establishing healthy, emotional and social relationships.

Street children, working and institutionalised children, thus form a special population at risk. Most of them come from socio-culturally deprived backgrounds which hinder healthy cognitive and language development. The families have been very uncongenial or absent for a long duration, resulting in the children's failure to develop trusting relationships with others. They, thus, seem to prefer to live in a hostile and alien world totally bereft of any emotional support. These children may become socially isolated and loners.

Many of them may indulge in gang activities and draw social support from their peers. Others may escape into the world of fantasy by watching movies. They hardly participate in play and game activities which facilitate healthy development. Working children and institutionalised children are prone to develop symptoms such as being emotionally and socially withdrawn, being anxious, miserable and unhappy, or become hostile and aggressive as a reaction to a hostile or indifferent environment.[4]

The needs of young children are different from those of adolescents. Young children need a secure emotional environment, with a caring substitute mother and a stimulating environment to facilitate cognitive and language development.

Adolescents need better models in terms of peer groups and an adult father substitute who is affectionate and understanding, yet capable of setting limits. There should be attractive and effective alternative activities to replace anti-social gang activities and escapist tendencies of watching movies.

All the categories of the at-risk populations described here need a specific package of total health care, including mental health care. This could be best provided by voluntary agencies which have their roots in the community, with the active involvement of the community. *The raising of social consciousness is necessary, and mental health professionals can provide the right kind of input in various interventive programmes in the long run.*

[4] The juvenile accused in the Nirbhaya rape case, for example.

The Convention of the Right of the Child in its 21 articles covers all the areas concerning healthy physical and psychosocial development of children. The Convention of the Right of the Child should be embraced whole-heartedly in spirit and practice in the developing countries, where there is an appalling lack of concern for, and exploitation of children.

Detrimental Effects and Intervention

- Detrimental effects vary according to the age, gender and contexts in which these occur.
- Parents are the ones who may cause the problems and may be able to intervene successfully.
- Various preventive measures are recommended but are not always successful.
- The interventions should be fine-tuned to the developmental context. No uniform intervention works.

PART II
CHILDREN AND SCHOOL

5

Education across the Nation A Dismal Scenario

A GOOD school programme/curriculum is the only consideration that merits attention in the Indian education scenario. This is true of most Asian and African countries among the developing nations. *In the Asian context, developmental psychology and educational practices have remained disparate disciplines much to the disadvantage of the vast child population. As a result, both child development and education have been largely neglected in the third world nations, especially India, despite the progress in higher education amongst a small group of relatively affluent elite population.*

In the West, education is based on sound educational practice in line with the current concepts and insights of developmental psychology. Developmental psychologists have segmentally focused on the domains of development such as motor, cognitive, language, emotional, social, moral and sexual development. The integration of these domains is emerging, albeit at a slow phase.

Indian teachers and parents believe that play is a waste of time and that time should in fact be spent most profitably in studies. Academic achievement is the only goal, the altar at which the child's creativity is sacrificed. Sadly, in India, 80-90 per cent children do not get quality education and those who get so-called good education in private schools too are subjected to very high academic pressure with no time for free play. There is complete neglect of psychosocial development and mental health of children.

ASER Reports (Rural)

Trends

Facilitated by Pratham, ASER (Annual Status of Education Report) is the annual survey of rural children, that has completed twelve years of survey in 2017.

Good News

- Student enrolment has increased. But variations are there between various States as well as gender.
- Infrastructure in general has improved, especially under the Sarva Shiksha Abhyan.
- Facilities such as drinking water, play area, toilets have improved.
- The best good news is that midday meals are provided for children in schools.

Bad News

- In all-India level there is **decline in attendance**, in some States showing sharp declines, as much as 73.4% to 70.9% in 2011.

- Over 50% have multi-grade classrooms nationally. That is several classes are clubbed together, managed by a single primary school teacher (classes 1 to 5) in rural India.
- **Reading levels** have declined in many States in north India. This decline is not seen in southern States.
- Arithmetic levels. Apart from three southern States, there has been overall decline (from 36.3% in 2010 to 29.9%, in class 5 from 70.9% to 61% in 2011).
- More children are moving to private schools with the hope of better education at a great cost to the families. This is more so because parents want them to go to English medium schools, as most government schools have the regional language as the medium of instruction. The thinking is, a child will get better access to opportunity if s/he knows English.

ASER 2012 (Rural)

- Enrolment at 6-14 continues to be high (96%) but *proportion of out of school has increased, especially girls.*
- Private school enrolment continues to rise in almost all States.
- Reading levels are of serious concern, with more than half of all children in standard V are found to be three grade levels below where they should be.
- Basic mathematics remains elusive to most primary school children across the nation.
- English Assessment: *in class VIII only 47% could read sentences.*
- Wide spread use of private schools and private tuitions has become a major trend.

- Proportion of small schools are on the rise.
- School facilities show improvement in pupil-teacher ratio (38.9% to 42.8%).
- 73% have drinking water.
- Toilet facilities, especially for girls have shown improvement.
- *Midday meals are provided in 87.1% of the schools.*

ASER 2013/14 (Rural)

Enrolment in 6-14 age group continues to be high at 96% in school. The proportion of 'out of schools girls' has declined since 2012.

- Nationally there is slight increase in private school enrolment along with paid tuition classes.
- *No improvement in reading level.*
- *Decline in basic arithmetic level.*

The silver lining is that there is improvement on several parameters of basic infrastructure and facilities. *Yet poor reading and mathematics reveals a deep fault line in our teaching methods.* It is not an exaggeration to say in the eight years of schooling, children hardly learn anything that can be claimed as an achievement. Suffice it to say we have failed our rural children. There is a need to turn the education system around by adopting child-centered play-way methods and bring about changes in the mindsets of teachers.

Critique: Almost a decade of time spent on surveys to provide us with excellent information, has not made any difference to education authorities. They could have each year tried developing intervention programmes at a small scale, keeping the survey results in mind.

Sadly, at the national level, a large percentage of children in Classes 3 to 5 in the government schools can only read Class 2 level books (35% in 2006, 37% in 2007 and 36% in 2008). Children whose mothers did not attend schools have far less proficiency and girls fare even worse. The State of Karnataka, where the author had opportunity to conducted research, has fared no better. A newspaper headline some time ago read,'91 per cent of Karnataka primary schools are headless'. Karnataka has better infrastructure but has fewer teachers with graduate degree and has the largest number of schools with no drinking water. A shocking statistic is that more than one third of the schools have no toilets, 60 per cent of the schools have no toilet facility for girls.

Researchers continue to be interested in collecting data, instead of providing intervention if possible. It is like declaring that there is malnutrition amongst children but not do anything about it. Even an intervention on a small scale, which actually benefits some children, is often more worthwhile instead of large scale surveys which provide only dry data with no benefit whatsoever to the children!

Education in India runs in two parallel streams. One is elitist education which follows the central syllabus catering to middle and upper-class families. The government-run schools often offer the State syllabus, mostly with the regional languages as medium of instruction. One would presume that the elitist group receives better quality education.

The author's experience as a Child Clinical Psychologist in the schools in the past three decades has been very disappointing, when viewed from the perspective of promotion of child development. Most elitist schools claim superiority based on better infrastructure and calibre of teachers and facilities for extracurricular activities. In contrast, all the schools for rural, tribal and other disadvantaged groups are provided very little.

ASER 2017

In the ASER Reports of 2006 to 2015 the focus was on basic numeracy and literacy skills in the age group of 5 to 14 years.

In the ASER 2017, the focus has rightly shifted to 14 to 18 years. This is due to near universal enrolment and automatic promotion. The sample surveyed was 30,000 children in the age range 14-18 years.

Results show, the enrolment to class VIII has doubled, that is, the from 11 million to 22 million, between 2006-2015. The same methodology as earlier has been used but the focus has gone 'beyond basics' to four key areas, namely: **Activity, Ability Awareness and Aspirations.**

Activity

Almost 80% are within the formal system and *14% out of it.*

About 5% take vocational courses of short duration, of less than 6 months and *40% of the children work in the agricultural sector.*

Ability

More girls drop out before reaching class VIII. This is a shocking development for India moving towards becoming a developed nation by 2030.

Literacy and numeracy skills continue to reflect the earlier trends. Interestingly, while reading skills in one's own language remains poor, 53% of the 14 year olds and 60% of the 18 year olds can read English! This is an aspirational trend.

Awareness

As many as 59% have no access to computer or internet. About 85% watch TV, 58% read newspapers and less than half listen to the radio.

Aspirations

As many as 75% have bank accounts of their own, 60% want to go for higher studies and 40% have no 'role models'. As vocational choice boys want to join the army or police force or become engineers. Girls chose teaching or nursing as their career choice.

To comment on the above findings, one may say that our children have aspirations and potential to create a new world. They need to be empowered with basic literacy, numeracy, vocational skills as well as opportunities. If we do not capitalise on the demographic dividend and educate our children, we will do great disservice to our nation.

ASER REPORT 2017: HARDLY FULL MARKS

% YOUTH CURRENTLY NOT ENROLED IN SCHOOL OR COLLEGE

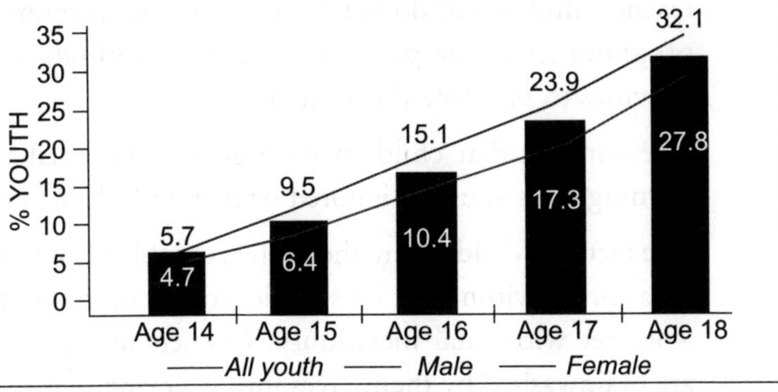

% YOUTH AT DIFFERENT READING LEVELS*

Reading level	Enroled in Std XII or below	Enroled in undergraduate or other	Not Enroled
Std II Level text	80.7	95.0	44.5
Std I level text	9.9	3.6	12.6
Word or below	9.5	1.3	42.9
Total	100	100	100

**By current enrolment status*

Learning deficits carry forward as 14 to 18-year-olds go from being adolescents to young adults

As a Child Psychologist, the author views all children as equally creative, imaginative and intelligent no matter what background they come from. Unfortunately, the elitist schools fail to be child-centred and child friendly. Having the right environment alone is not enough. *To have the* ***right attitude*** *to childhood among parents and teachers alike are necessary.*

Banes of Our Education System

- Emphasis on academic achievement from early classes onwards can have adverse effect on normal psychosocial development in all the domains such as physical, cognitive, language, emotional, social, moral and sexual development.
- Emphasis on teacher-centred approach, whether teachers undergo or do not undergo numerous training programmes to prepare more charts, methods and activities to promote the academic skills.
- The concept that children have greater potential for learning than adults is ignored or met with disbelief.
- The fact that children are themselves capable of creating a learning environment far superior to that of the adults – is met with total incredulity. Teachers and parents are brainwashed by themselves into believing that they know what to teach and how to teach.
- Neglect of State languages and mother tongues of children of hundreds of languages,with authorities oblivious to the fact these are anchors to cultural heritage and identity of these children.

'Teachers teach, psychologists know: can the two meet?' asks eminent educationist Prof Krishna Kumar.

Psychologists hold overall development of the child as of utmost importance, be it at home or at school. However, this

Weight of the Schoolbag

School bag: Heaviest burden on students of unaided schools

Survey reveals students of govt. schools have the lightest load, averaging 3.7 kg

WEIGHT INCREASES WITH EACH YEAR

Class	KV	CBSE	ICSE	State-aided	State-unaided	State govt.
I	2.2	3.7	3.4	4.1	3.2	1.8
V	4.3	5.3	4.5	4.7	[illegible]	3.6
VII	6.1	6.5	6.5	5.2	7.6	4.9
X	8.0	5.7	5.0	4.3	6.7	5.5
XII	8.3	4.6	NA	NA	NA	NA

Full School Bag and Empty Brain!

development occurs in a particular culture. Unless the cultural context is taken into account, we are doomed to failure. India's education focuses on teaching methods and adopts a teacher-centred approach. Sound psychological understanding as to how a child learns is crucial.

Obviously, children in government schools do not get quality education. One would assume that the elite group gets it. Unfortunately, this is not true. Here too, the teacher-centred approach is practised, placing even greater burden on children, depriving them of all joys of childhood. *Sadly, the school has become a part of the service industry, focusing on generating more wealth than promoting children's overall development.* The new-fangled, much-touted 'techno school' franchises even work against children from a developmental perspective and hence need to be and should be shut down. Likewise, the preschools that insist on advanced academic language and maths skills and home work at the cost of free play need to be banned.

Reasons for Poor Literacy and Poor Quality of Education

Historical Factors

An important historical factor is the *caste system* which is deeply rooted in the national ethos. The caste system in the past and, to a certain extent, in the present too, promotes an elitist approach to education. Upper caste men, traditionally the Brahmin and to certain extent Kshatriyas, had opportunities for education in the recent past while it was denied to women and people belonging to the Scheduled Caste and Tribes.

To add to this bias, Brahmins used Sanskrit which further alienated most of the people who did not know Sanskrit. The language factor operated in the traditional Muslim education system also. Mullahs used Arabic for teaching. This came in the way of mass education to a large segment of the population in India. Buddhism, in contrast, adopted the language of the people and promoted mass education in Myanmar and Sri Lanka.

Another historical factor is that, under the colonial rule, the British in India supported the expansion of higher education at the cost of 'mass education'. Amartya Sen talks of appalling neglect of mass education at the altar of higher education (Jayakumar Anagol 2003). Unfortunately, even after independence, the momentum in favour of higher education continued to operate. The neglect of quality mass education continues, although quantitatively, mass education has reached many more people.

Community Response

It is generally believed that illiterate parents do not want their children to be educated. This is a misconception, as most illiterate parents do want their children to have education and a chance to better their lives, an opportunity which they themselves did not have. However, other factors also enter into a poor community response. For example, girl children are kept out of school due to reasons such as the need to attend to household chores, not having female teachers, absence of toilets in the schools and the belief that a girl need not be educated as she is not going to be a bread winner and will go to another home; hence not worth the investment. But studies also show that even the illiterate mothers do want their daughters to study.

School System

Deep fault lines run in the school system. These are *high dropout* rates and *absenteeism.* The high dropout rates are related to exaggerated enrolment rates reported by teachers. High absenteeism amongst teachers and children, regional needs of farming communities where extra hands are needed at certain times of the year, and local festivals and village shandies also take their toll as the children accompany their parents on these occasions.

The above problems are not irremediable. *In Kerala, for example, 100 per cent of the children complete five years of schooling. In contrast, it is only 38 per cent in Bihar. Among the Scheduled Caste and tribal children, it is even lower.*

Economic Factors

Conditions of the schools continue to be very poor even after decades of Operation Blackboard. The cost of primary education seems to be one of the causes. Yet *Himachal Pradesh had earlier set a model in the past of high achievement for the entire country because of the political will to do so.*

Poor Teacher Motivation and Poor Teaching Methods

The attendance of the teachers is low. Teachers often reach late and leave early. They often do not hold classes. This reflects poor motivation on the part of the teachers. *Motivation is further compromised by the government asking the teachers to do other non-teaching duties.* About 150 days of 200-250 days, the teachers are being given additional unrelated duties such as elections, census, collection of food rations for school, collection of uniforms, books and their distribution.

In Finland, where the education system is considered the best in the world; the schools have shorter hours, 1:20 teacher pupil ratio, less focus on syllabus and more child-centred methods of promoting creativity and imagination. Most importantly, the new parents have gifted books to be read to children!

When I say that we can impart all the required scholastic skills through play, the teachers and parents are aghast. Teachers, however, may agree in theory but in practice do not know how it can be done.

Here is an experiment I had conducted in HD Kote (Heggada Devana Kote is a taluk in Mysore) to prove this point.

I have demonstrated the methods of bridging the gap between education and child development in two samples of 1,200 children from Class 1 to 9 in 15 rural schools run by the Education Department. These methods are described in detail in Chapters 17,18 and 19.

Promotion of Psychosocial Development of Rural Children

The objective of the programmes was to evolve and evaluate the promotion of psycho-social development of 1,200 rural and 800 tribal school children, of whom 1,088 and 306 had psychological assessments before and after the interventions.

The interventions carried out elsewhere in the country are mostly segmental in nature and mostly attempt to enhance the performance in the curricular subjects. The programmes also pay scant attention to evaluating the effectiveness of programmes. The present work adopts a comprehensive approach for the promotion of all the domains of development such as cognitive, language, emotional, social skills along with creativity. It also aims at objective evaluation of the outcome of the intervention using psychological tests. As the programme covers all the children in the target population, it is termed as **universal intervention.**

Working with children in small groups, for an hour or more each day of the week, the stimulation programme consisted of a package of activities which adopted a child-to-child approach. The programme made use of play, games, artwork, number and word games, drama, song and dance activities to promote fine and gross motor, cognitive, language, emotional, social and moral development. Apart from games, innovative ways to promote creativity and 'life skills' education with older children were carried out. The programme was carried out with the involvement of teachers, villagers and older children teaching younger children. Results indicate the following:

a. The intervention programme produced significant improvement as measured on the performance on tests of **attention, memory, intelligence, arithmetic, language and creativity**—on objective assessment.

b. There were variations in improvement across age, gender and caste.

c. The intervention consisted of 25-30 one-hour sessions per day, for six days a week.

d. The teacher and community involvement rendered the programme more effective. At times, when teachers were unavailable, the grandmother, village youth, cook or an older child took charge to monitor the programme. This shows that the programme can be run by anyone who is interested and motivated to do it. In fact, these interventions showed improvements superior to that done by our team. (Geetha: Personal Communication).

e. Dysfunctional schools and homes appeared to lead to poor academic performance and mental health.

f. The intervention can be replicated across schools in urban slums and rural India and across other developing nations and the disadvantaged sections of the developed nations.

The key components of the successful interventions were:

- Children being the resource for their learning.
- Child-centered play way methods.
- No traditional instructional methods focusing only on academic skills.
- Evaluation using pre- and post-assessment on psychological tests to assess the efficacy as well as to monitor and improve upon the methods if necessary and to fine tune these to suit age, gender and grade differences.

We attempted to capitalise on what the children already knew. We asked them to speak in their own language and got other children to translate these for us. Language carries a cultural heritage of the specific caste, religion, tribal and other cultural groups. This broadens our knowledge of that community. We carried out these by encouraging them to tell stories, sing songs and dances that they already knew. It is very important to preserve the use of the mother tongue of the child. Mother tongue carries the cultural heritage and the real identity of the child. It is a sad state of affairs when the child speaks and learns only one language, namely English because of the status accorded to it by society and enable the youth in achieving upward social mobility.

A sub-sample study where all the teachers were previously trained in this joyful learning programme called 'Nali Kali'[5] was done. Assessment was carried out in those schools where no improvement occurred after 3 months. But they did show comparable improvement like rest of our groups, after our intervention programme. This suggests that the Nali Kali, as practised by the teachers, was quite ineffective.

Implications

The study has several implications. The first is that children can be the resource for promotion of their own psychological development and this is mediated by age, gender and social class.

5 Developed in 1995 by teachers in Karnataka's Mysore district, the Nali Kali strategy adopted creative learning practices to help retain children in school and bring in those not attending school.
Child competencies were pegged to a learning ladder and the learning process was organised into milestones providing every child the opportunity to assess his or her own progress.
The initiative has helped improve enrolment, particularly of girls, and has been expanded to cover more areas within Mysore and 10 more districts in the State. Plans are underway to extend the initiative across the State.

Approaches to development should be inclusive of intervention of mental health and disabilities. However, an integrated approach involving the health, education and welfare sectors is equally important in reaching out to children.

Children as the Resource

Promotion of child development in the contemporary context of developmental psychology emphasises approaches which are creative, flexible and child-centered. In developed nations, especially for schools catering to the middle and upper strata of society, such approaches are widely practised. But these

Comparison of the Traditional and the Preferred Methods:

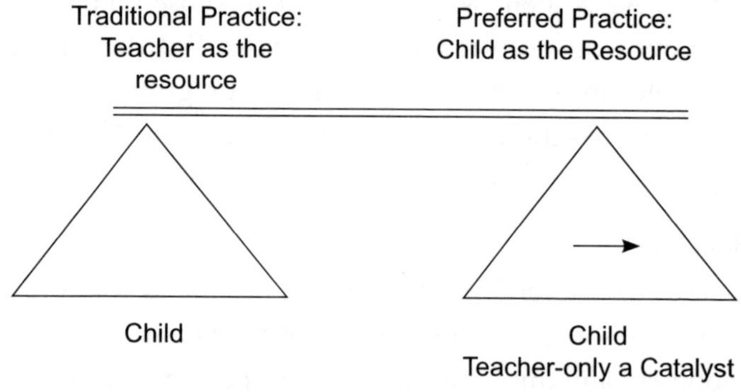

are expensive in terms of the toys and equipment and are manpower-intensive. In developing countries and in the disadvantaged populations across the world, such schooling remains beyond their dreams. *The rural and urban government schools in India are unlikely to ever provide such educational facilities to 'their children' in the near or far future.*

In India, teachers are expected to use child-friendly methods in teaching while *very few teachers are themselves child-friendly.*

They choose to follow traditional instructional methods, where teaching is unilateral, from the teacher to the child. It is essential to make them aware of the following:

The Traditional and the Preferred Methods:

To conclude, there is a need to create awareness among the parents and teachers that play should be the natural medium of instruction. *It should be child-centered and child is the creator of his enriched environment that he shares with the other children. Play provides shortcuts to enhanced scholastic skills. But the most important idea is an empowered learner has high self esteem as he makes his way through the world. There is a need to appreciate mother tongue, regional language and English equally. Child is a natural learner of multiple languages in India. Languages provide cultural rootedness and identity.*

6

Peer Difficulties

THE SCHOOL authorities and teachers play an important role in the lives of children. The impact of these may vary across ages from nursery, primary, middle and high school levels. A young child is most vulnerable to the strange children and adults whom he meets outside his secure and comfortable home, when he joins school.

The younger the child, harder it is to enter this new world of strangers. About the teachers, he has some ideas as parents would have talked to him about them. But the other children are in an area which is totally new to him. No one talks about them. For a single child especially, this can be a very rewarding or a very threatening experience.

Good peer relations pave the way for pro-social and mature interactions. It permits the child to explore a new and adventurous world in the company of friends. This is perhaps more risk-taking and exploratory. He is introduced to a new world away from home.

My impression of how learning and social change gets rooted was acquired when I was working in the Ashram Schools (residential schools for tribal children) in HD Kote, noting the way the children displayed their compassion and pro-social behaviour. Older boys/girls took care of the younger ones in helping them to get ready, groom the hair, and generally taking over the parental duties as if they were their younger siblings.

Other dramatic instances of pro-social behaviour emerged out of the famous free midday meal programmes in urban and rural government schools. Apart from increasing school attendance, this has contributed to much more mixing of children belonging to different castes. It is generally believed that children learn about caste, class, gender discriminations from the adults around them. It is the peer group that allows them to see these in a different light.

Peer Problems

Despite positive contributions of peer groups, often peers can pose very difficult problems.

Bullying

Bullying of weaker, younger, timid or those with disabilities or even with eccentricities is encountered frequently in schools. Victims are often threatened with even more severe punishment if they report the bullying to their parents or teachers. In the Western world there is awareness and these are discussed in the class rooms to reduce such instances. In India, no one talks about bullying in schools and school authorities often deny that bullying exists in 'their' school.

Programmes to Counter Bullying: In India, teachers often overlook these events and take it as common practice that all the children should get used to. The targeted child may develop psychological problems such as anxiety and as an extreme step, may refuse to go to school.

Callous School Authorities

Pruthvi, a nine-year-old boy, is in fourth standard. His family consists of his parents and an elder brother. He was born premature. Because of his soft nature, he was a victim of frequent peer bullying. Three of his schoolmates regularly used sharp pencils to prick his head, whenever he got his hair cut.

One day, while in the class, those three kids gave him a sharp pencil and asked him to poke it into the eyes of the boy sitting next to Pruthvi, which he refused to do as the boy was his best friend. When the class got over those boys followed Pruthvi. They threw a plastic wire around his neck from behind. He caught it to stop from falling. Immediately they threw another rope and began pulling him from behind. He caught hold of both the string and the rope and struggled to get rid of their hold. The fight went on for some time. Seeing a teacher coming, the bullies ran away.

Pruthvi went home bleeding all over. He was taken to the hospital immediately and got treated. He was hospitalised for a month. The parents were afraid of sending the child to school. They spoke to the management to change his section, away from those three kids. The management told them to take away their child from their school.

The parents had not at first complained against the school. Now they took the help of the police. When the police intervened and warned the school authorities, those three students were put in three other sections, separately.

—Contributed by Rajalakshmi

Deliberately Destroying Relationships

Some children enjoy intrigues and they tend to make up things, tell lies and make children mistrust each other just for the fun of it. The children, who manipulate, often do it for fun. The children who manipulate perhaps learn it from adults at home or others they encounter. All children need close friends. Breaking up of relationships is traumatic to many. There are instances of young children feeling let down even when their friends are sent to another division (class).

Scapegoating

Often, in a classroom setting, if one child cheats or steals, other children may gang up and accuse another child who is totally innocent. Mostly, teachers and students deliberately blame a particular child for no fault of his, not even considering that they could be wrong. This is an exceedingly harmful practice as far as the falsely accused child is concerned.

Physical Harming and Ragging

Some children, often those who are exposed to physical punishment at home or at school, may take out their anger on other children for trivial reason or even without provocation. The targeted child feels completely helpless when all the adults overlook this as just horse play among children. To tease a child mercilessly, much to the amusement of other children and even amongst the teachers, is a common practice. This happens in an exaggerated fashion in residential hostels, where the victim is totally at the mercy of vindictive hostel mates.

Refusing to go to School

It was in the month of October. This is a scene from class six. Deepa was one among the few students who had not done the Kannada home-work that day. The teacher got angry and generously used her teaching tool, namely, the stick. The rest of the class enjoyed the show, by laughing merrily.

Deepa did not tell her parents about this 'insulting incident'. Since that day, she began bunking classes quite often. Till then she was regular. Her non-homework days became a general phenomenon and being beaten in the class even more a regular process. The problem reached her parents also. The mother went to the school and apologised for her daughter's flaws. After some days, Deepa began to cry bitterly, trembling at the time of going to school. Day by day, it became a nightmare for her and a greater problem to her parents. Her situation began worsening. Parents were unable to help her. They took her to temples and several poojas were offered. The annual exams came. Somehow, they were able to convince her to write the exams and she did and got through.

She successfully entered the 7th standard. Everything was going on smoothly, till October, when Deepa again began getting nightmares about going to school. The same cycles repeated, with more severity. Parents took her to alternate healers and counselling centre also, in addition to the earlier ones. Finally, Deepa revealed the root of her fear to her counsellor after several sessions. Then, the process of making Deepa strong enough to face the situation began.

The counsellor spoke to the school authorities, and also to the parents. Parents understood the child's situation and got ready to help her. Deepa was made to enter the school, fighting her fears with gradual steps. Getting into the uniform, carrying her school bag, leaving home, reaching the van stop, getting into the van, reaching the school gate, entering the premises, going near the class, entering the classroom... like this she was encouraged to move gradually, with the help of her parents. Mother took her to her friends' places quite frequently. Her friends' help was also sought. Her peers also were ready to help her.

Deepa was interested in drawing. This was used as another tool to overcome her fear, simultaneously with the other aids. The humiliating incident was mocked at through her drawings, making cartoon-ike pictures of the incident with various elements of humour added to it. This made her strong sense of fear into a funny, laughing matter for herself. That is how Deepa was able to laugh at the incident that had happened more than a year ago, which was the root cause of her present state.

With several of such efforts, Deepa was finally able to attend her classes fearlessly and the last one she did was her Kannada class. That was her victory against her toughest fears and the all-round pressures! She won her battle to the extent that on their valedictory day, she greeted her Kannada teacher also, shaking hand with her. She continued in the same school, she doesn't carry any vengeance against her Kannada teacher. She is enjoying her schooling once again!

—Contributed by Rajalakshmi

Sexual Abuse and Molestation

This is an issue much in the news. Curiosity about sex and related aspects is natural. In India, sexuality is a subject which is not discussed openly even among adults, let alone children. Sexuality is a tabooed subject. Teachers do not like the idea of having sex education in school. Parents mostly try to avoid thinking or talking about sexuality of their child. Consequently, the children obtain knowledge of sex through unhealthy channels such as pornography on internet, movies (Indian movies often show blatantly sexual content) and picture books and magazines. Of course, word-of-mouth by the other children is a major source of information. The idea of sexuality as it occurs around puberty is a normal phase of development. Along with bodily changes, heightened sexuality too occurs. An adolescent at puberty passes through three phases of sexuality, self sex (masturbation), same sex (homosexuality) and heterosexuality. In the schools all the three behaviours may manifest. If the opportunity arises, children do experiment with sex. However, irresponsible or hurtful sex needs to be avoided.

> Two children from an orphanage were brought to our centre by the orphanage staff in great panic. Lakshmi, aged seven years and Santosh, aged six years were reported to have locked themselves in a classroom. When told to come out they did and revealed that they had removed their clothes and were looking at each other. When gently spoken to and asked what had happened, the children separately narrated their experiences. The new entrant to the orphanage, a fourteen-year-old boy, had told them to do this, because it was fun! The two children were then told why this action would upset other children and staff of the institution. They were gently persuaded not to repeat it again and the staff were educated regarding how sexual exploitation was normal and not to be taken as a great offence or sin. As the fourteen-year-old was a repeat offender, the orphanage was told that he needed to be sent to child psychiatric consultation. But they, instead, chose to transfer him to another orphanage. This meant the problems would continue in the new orphanage too. This was not a solution!

There is a great need for awareness and prevention of sexual exploitation that can hurt a child psychologically or physically. A compassionate and caring parent or a teacher can make a world of difference to the handling of issues of sexuality by the children. Avoiding any discussion on them at home and school is invitation to sexual abuse. If the parents discuss the issues in a free and fair manner, the child can confide even the worst-case scenario to them. Then handling the trauma becomes doable.

Gang Activities

Some children form gangs and hang out together. They may be absent from schools (truancy). They come to school on time and return home on time but are not found in classrooms. These children may steal, destroy property and show aggressive behaviour. But even worse, they may indulge in drug and alcohol intake. Addictions take hold of youngsters easily. From then onward it is a downhill trend. Often the parents do not discover about it, till it is much too late. Teachers may not notice that the children are absent. The gangs tend to receive more members as what they do is enjoyable. Having a home which is full of parental conflicts may trigger these behaviours.

Being part of a Gang

Amir came from a village in Ananthpur district to Bengaluru as his mother believed in an urban education system. He joined LKG in Bengaluru when he was four years old. For this, he had to leave his parents and his only tiny younger sister, who he was very fond of. He stayed with his grandparents. His new house was full of highly-educated aunts and uncles. His grandparents and the remaining adults were strict disciplinarians.

The child was running out of the house during sleep, ever since he came to the city. So, they had to keep the house keys hidden from Amir. This behaviour was not at all seen when he went to visit his parents.

He was an average student, but his foster family expected a top grade from him all the time. The child was beaten severely, kept without food on the days following poor results.

He had no complaints against any of these. He honestly believed that all these punishments were needed for his 'good'.

He was in 10th standard when his school complained against him to his grandparents. The reason for the complaint was, Amir along with three of his friends, had destroyed several items belonging to the school premises. They had broken all the windows and doors, bulbs, and electrical fittings. He was sternly beaten and his parents were summoned to take him back.

The mother took him to a counselling centre. Once the counsellor gained his faith, Amir revealed why they broke windows. It was for the simple desire (ambition?) that the boys wanted to be remembered by the school for ever. They wanted to be in the list of eternally remembered students and planned to do something special to achieve this. They got this idea to have names etched in the history of their school!

The school authorities naturally complained to the Police; they in turn informed the children's parents/guardians and invited them for a meeting. One can only imagine the rest!

—Contributed by Rajalakshmi

A good understanding between the home and school about the children is the remedy. The children's undesirable behaviour can be eliminated if discovered early by the cooperative efforts of the parents and teachers.

7

Teacher Fault Lines

CHILDREN DIFFER in their abilities related to intelligence, language, attention and memory skills. But most children fall within the normal range or in the average range. There can be a small percentage of those who are very dull or very bright. So, no child in a normal classroom is backward because of lack of intelligence. But teachers believe that **only some children are bright and capable of being good in studies.**

Children differ in their personalities or temperament. Some are quiet, withdrawn (Tamasik) and laid back; some are very active, friendly, talkative and some even aggressive (Rajasik) while some others are cheerful, happy and helpful (Satvik). Some children take time to warm up, some are easy to manage while some are very difficult to care for. These children relate to adults as well as other children differently. **Teachers in India somehow believe all children are similar in their response**

to punishments and rewards. But children do differ from each other.

Praise and Punishments

Some teachers praise children who are their favourites, because of looks, school performance, familiarity, caste, gender and such other characteristics and show partiality to them. This may encourage the ones who are praised but the other children get very upset by this obvious partiality and start resenting the teachers as well as their favourite students. When the teacher compares the other children to their favourite child, the atmosphere in the classroom gets vitiated, leading to unpleasant behaviour due to jealousy.

Similarly, the teachers also tend to single out a few children to punish all the time. This not only make the targeted children upset, it also leads other children to treat them badly.

The teachers' belief, that some children are entirely 'good' and some are entirely 'bad' is a mistaken notion. All children are bundles of good and bad qualities. No one is wholly good or bad.

Teachers in general mean well towards children they teach. But their methods of teaching may not be appropriate. Most teachers believe that they know everything and children know nothing. Consequently, they repeatedly teach what they think is needed for children to pass in the exams, ask them to copy what is written on the board or in the book. But no attempt is made by the teacher to find out if the child has understood what is being taught or written.

This teacher-centred one-way instructional method without checking if it is being understood by the child is the biggest problem of teaching method used by most of the teachers in India. This has been the conventional approach in all our schools.

The above approach, in addition, does not allow children to be playful, be talkative or be asking questions. They are expected only to listen quietly, answer questions and not participate in classroom discussion. Anything other than obedient silence is met with severe punishment, often with a stick.

Without realising teachers snub the children, humiliate them, shove and push them around, pinch or pull their ears without meaning to hurt them. Children need to be respected at all times.

Asking Questions!

Dinesh, an-eleven-year old boy, was threatened with Transfer Certificate from the school. His parents were called to meet the school authorities. The parents were worried and went to apologise on their child's behalf for the unknown crime the child had committed.

'He asks irrelevant questions to teachers. By doing so, he disturbs the whole class and embarrasses the teacher. He enjoys it', reported the school authorities.

The parents wished to know more in detail so that they could understand the situation and correct the child. 'He asks "what is reproduction?" when the teacher takes her class on "Reproduction". Is it right on his part? Do you think a good student should do this?' Parents apologised and promised, 'It won't happen in future'. They took the child to a counsellor to mend his ways!

—*Contributed by Rajalakshmi*

Teachers believe that children cannot and will not learn unless they are punished. They take the 'spare the rod'-dictum seriously. They do not consider punishment as bad even though legally, they are not permitted to use corporal punishment.

Enriched learning materials, though provided by the government to children, is often not used at all. The reasons given are:

The attractive, expensive, or even inexpensive, material will be damaged by children as they are playful and naturally destructive. Be it art or craft material, books, games and other play and instructional materials, musical instruments are kept under lock and key and never given to the children. May be the fear of being answerable to higher-ups. The idea behind it is that these materials are too good to be given to children! *This is one of the major psychological blocks in the mindset of the teachers that the good materials should be 'protected' from the destructive children!* Consequently, children are not given even the basic requirements of play, enjoyment and learning in the classroom settings. It is like buying a doll and not giving it to the child because it will be damaged. Hence the doll is kept in a showcase where the child can see it every day but cannot have it. It is like saying 'Do not give food to the child because it gets finished if he eats it!'

The teacher fault lines are:

- Individual differences among children in their abilities, skills and temperaments are not paid attention to
- Indiscriminate use of punishment
- Partiality towards some children
- Teacher-centred approach where learning is by Rote and comprehension of the content is not paid any attention to
- Punishment is the best tool of teaching
- Any material provided for enriching the learning experience are not given to children as they are likely to destroy them

An observation of display of aggression in rural schools: In one of my sessions on child development and mental health for the teachers, about 40 of them, I posed the following questions (based on the World Health Organisation categories of aggression):

Q. How many children destroy school or personal properties/objects of others?

Ans: None

Q. How many are aggressive towards the teachers?

Ans: None

Q. How many teachers are aggressive towards them?.... beat or punish them?

Ans: Candid answers, **'Most of us!'**

If children show no aggression, what provokes the teachers to punish them? Newspapers are replete with examples of teacher brutality for

- Not doing homework
- Not learning the poems by heart
- Not knowing by heart the multiplication tables
- Not answering questions
- Coming late
- Not groomed properly

The list of minor issues is endless but are treated by teachers as if these are criminal acts with criminal intent.

My question is why are we so hard on children in schools? What right does an outsider have to hurt someone else's child?

Children's physical safety is not seen as the responsibility of the teachers. The teachers believe that safety in the school surrounding too is the responsibility of the parents. There are numerous reports of children's safety being endangered physically and sexually in the school premises. These are perpetuated by the teachers, other staff, drivers and others.

The school authorities and teachers believe that children's safety is not their concern.

To summarise, according to the teachers and the school authorities **only education** in terms of information inputs is a matter of concern to them. The other aspects of making the child happy and an empowered learner or promoting the overall development is of no consequence to the teachers. Only the scholastic achievement is of paramount importance. Only this end result is important. The means of reaching is once again overlooked as they persist in adopting teacher-centred, rote learning interspersed with punishment.

The tragedy of education in India is in the faulty mindsets of the people. But let me assure you, most of them truly believe in the system they follow unquestioningly. They do not understand why the children do not learn. The teachers too are good people, shaped by adult expectations and find children a species beyond their comprehension. But should the teachers and children have such an insurmountable barrier between them?

A Play Home or Just Another 'School'?

Chitra was a two-and-half year old girl when her parents, staying in a new extension of a growing city, took care of her with sensitivity. They put her in a nearby playschool to facilitate her play with children of her age. She happily went to school.

After returning from school the second day, Chitra began to play with her toys repeating, 'No! Chup! I'll put you in the dog's room!' The mother and the grandmother observed this play continuing daily after school for some more days. After two weeks, the girl refused to go to school.

The parents went and spoke to the playschool authorities. Their initial response was denial. Then gradually they put the blame on the 'Ayahs'. When the parents caught a teacher red-handed saying it, the principal confessed, saying, 'What to do, many parents say that we have to threaten their children, make them fearful. Or else he/she doesn't listen to the parents. You are the only parents saying not to do so'.

After a week the child began to stammer. The parents were naturally alarmed. Schooling on alternate days was practised for some weeks. Family members thought that it was the high time to start preparing the child to face world's reality. The child was encouraged to express her burdens through drawings, enacting the school with family members and playing with her toys. These activities had a great impact. Gradually her stammering decreased and the schooling days were increased. Chitra began to attend to her school regularly, though home is her most favourite place!

—Contributed by Rajalakshmi

The above example, reveals how children at different ages, preschool, primary, middle and high schools are faced with different set of problems from the rest of the children and the teachers. These often are brought to the notice of the teachers and school authorities. Sometimes, rarely though, teachers mediate and help. However, many a time, the parents too are spoken too harshly and humiliated. Sometimes parents themselves side with the teachers, thus leading to isolation and helplessness in the child. Our children need better support and communication between parents and teachers. This will be discussed in the next chapter.

8

Collusion and Collision between Teachers and Parents

THERE ARE many practices that are detrimental to the child's learning. In India, these are well known practices. These are home work, tuitions, learning by rote and examinations and grades are viewed as the ultimate indicators of success. The basic assumption the developmental psychologists have is that, most children have average intelligence. If the children come from literate families, teaching that goes on in normal school hours should be able to empower the child with required grade-related to scholastic skills or the 3 Rs (Reading, wRiting and aRithmetic). If these are achieved in the primary school level, this lays a good foundation for high school and later on to college. Most of us have been fortunate to have experienced this in our childhood.

Home Work

If the basic subjects are taught properly in the class over 6-8 hours a day, where is the need for homework? If the child understands what is going on in the class, there is no need for doing more of the same at home as well. After long hours at school, the child is forced to do homework. Often different teachers give different homework, without realising the total number of hours it takes to complete all of them. Why should the child feel happy or be attentive when completing this dreary task? Sometimes he hides the homework, sometimes he does it carelessly only to get into trouble next day at school. The mother (mostly it is the mother) who feels responsible and takes over the task of either doing it herself or sitting endless hours, persuading the child to complete it. This becomes a daily routine, leading to frustrating and angry interaction between the mother and the child.

IS IT NECESSARY that the mother has to help?

It is totally incomprehensible why the mother should have any role in completing the homework. *If a child cannot do the homework on his own, it should not be given at all. What does the teacher do at school then?* At present, there is collusion between the teachers and the parents. Teachers feel that mothers should contribute to teaching. If no homework is given, instead being happy, the mother gets concerned that no homework is given. The final outcome is the long hours spent in homework, which is hard on the child and the mother, it also TAKES AWAY the time when the child, in fact, should be playing. If the mother spends the same amount of time taking the child out to the park, telling him stories, talking to him, playing with the sibling, it would enhance his overall development. This is the description of 'quality time' by the mother that enhances healthy mother-child interactions. Thus, home work deprives the child of 'quality time' with the family as well. **Do we need homework? We do not!**

Tuitions

These are additional classes taken outside the regular class hours, generally on the basis of payment. Most often it is the school/class teacher himself who takes these classes. More often, the tuitions are given to large groups of children in cramped places, usually in the homes of the teachers. These may last anywhere from 1 to 4 hours. But what is important to note is that these are simply repetition of what goes on in classrooms during the day. The difference now is that both teacher and children are tired and worn out because of this burden.

The benefit for the teacher is the extra income and satisfaction to the parent, that 'I am buying additional help for my child'. Rarely, if fortunate, a child may end up with a good teacher. But mostly, it is repetitive rote learning. Of course, rote learning needs repeated instructions! The tragedy is that while the teacher and the parents are happy – the children are generally unhappy about tuitions.

Homework or any other scholastic work for that matter has become the only subject/topic of conversation between parents and child/children. A child may learn to use this to gain and retain parents' attention by not doing the work either himself or at all. He may expect the mother to do it on his behalf.

Class work – if a child cannot complete in the class it has to be completed at home.

School gives Home Work

Tuition teacher gives Home Work

Study at home (to be able to 'write well' in exams)

In a day of 24 hours–when can a child breathe some fresh air?

Often when the child cannot finish homework at school, he brings it home. Then he has to go to tuition as well as complete those assignments. Then parents insist that he studies all the time. When does the child play and enjoy normal childhood?

The tuition teacher might even have an idea what questions may come in the examinations. Thus, the child may spend the entire effort in preparing for examinations.

These are other forms of practices for higher classes such as coaching classes. Yet another poor educational technology is the use of so called 'guides'. These are badly written diluted cheap editions of text books. These are often full of typographical, grammatical and content-related errors, which the pupil is expected to learn by rote and reproduce in the examinations. Once again production of 'guides' is a lucrative practice.

All the above practices are encouraged by the teachers,

parents and teaching business houses. All of these add up to good deal of loss of money to the family and with no benefit to the child at all. In conclusion, the fact is, all the above come in the way of creativity and learning, taking away time from play, an essential component for the overall development of a child. But it is unfortunate that Indian parents, teachers and the school system collude in creating this exceedingly counterproductive learning environment.

Collision between Teachers and Parents

There are instances of collision between the parents and teachers. One of the major example is the 25 per cent admission of government school children of 6 to 14 years of age to private schools under the provision of Right to Education Act. Private schools resist it because it means loss of income; also fear of poor percentage and they demand money from the poor parents under other guises such as sports, extra books etc.

But even more saddening is the lack of 'social conscience' in the private profit-making school system. It considers children from lower classes and poor families are unworthy of being in the same classroom as the children who are privileged from birth. Those admitted to the private schools under duress by the education department are more often than not discriminated against, isolated and humiliated.

They are kept in separate classrooms with teachers who give them the same treatment as government schools.

There are instances where they are made to wear wrist bands to demarcate them from other children. Sometimes, the difference in the social class and discrimination makes the children leave these very schools which they had strived for. They are allotted a separate classroom with regional language teacher. This ensures that they will never catch up with children with the English medium instruction.

As usual, these are instances of corruption negating the aims of this RTE provision. The Block Education Officer colludes with influential parents who can afford private schools, to deny seats to those who are rightfully entitled to these seats. Delays, oversights, indifference on part of the education department makes very large number of seats fall vacant. Though 20 lakh seats should be filled under this Act, only 5-6 lakhs are being filled up at present.[6]

If the private schools and education department take a more compassionate approach to the deserving government school children, RTE programme could be a shining beacon to an egalitarian society. Instead, the private schools take legal recourse to keep the poor children out.

The other major issue is that of safety of children in schools. The education departments and parents place the onus of responsibility on the schools: private or otherwise. But the school authorities try their best to evade it. **Right to Education and safety of children are moral questions. No amount of legal recourses can show a way out.**

Right to Education – Some Observations

The amounts are fixed to obtain an eligibility certificate for RTE admissions in all the concerned offices.

Is government admitting the poor quality of education in government schools?

The cost is supposed to be borne by the government for all RTE admissions, but has not reached the concerned schools even after two years in most cases.

---

[6] The Right of Children to Free and Compulsory Education (RTE) Act, 2009, represents the consequential legislation envisaged under Article 21-A, means that every child has a right to full time elementary education of satisfactory and equitable quality in a formal school which satisfies certain essential norms. This Act of the Parliament of India enacted on 4 August 2009, describes the modalities of the importance of free and compulsory education for children between 6 and 14 in India under Article 21-A of the Indian Constitution.

There are also schools taking children – without filtering – and giving concession in fees, considering the family income.

Both the issues rest on the conscience of the adults involved – as moral neglect leads to deprivation and physical threats to the safety of children.

A Challenge that Opens Possibilities for the Children

The medium of instruction is a bug bear for the Indian education system.

There are those who advocate English as the medium of instruction and there are those who wish to promote regional languages as it is generally done in all the government schools. It should not be English or Indian language. It should be both. Knowledge of English opens many more doors of access to information and better job opportunities. Upward mobility is the right of every individual in the country and should not be denied to anybody.

On the other hand, knowing your own language (reading and writing) keeps one culturally rooted. The fact is that even a three-year-old can speak three Indian languages along with English if he is exposed to it. Working knowledge in several languages facilitates brain development, enhancing not only development of language but also cognition as the latest research on bilingualism in children. Children can learn languages with great ease unlike adults, who have to struggle for language acquisition. The parents from poorest of the poor home want their children to learn English. The author's own experiments detailed in the next chapter supports that it is possible.

Some Exercises to be Better Teachers and Parents

1. Try to recall some of your childhood memories. Pick up the happy as well as sad memories. Try to view the

reasons for them being happy and/or sad. (With such analysis or introspection, try to understand the child in front of you.)

2. Try to watch a child doing anything, without assessing or correcting him. Try to imitate the child's act and know if the child in you is alive and/or if you can understand the child as he is.
3. Try to stand in the shoes of a child and feel the child. For example, when a parent casually talks about the child (above 2 or 3 years year) bed wetting to a friend, or a teacher mentioning the stupidity of the child in front of others. On such occasions, if you imagine yourself in place of the child, you may never repeat such conversation. Remember, a child also feels the insult and expects and deserves respect.
4. Try to behave in a way you expect your child to behave. And the child learns mostly by watching the adults around him. Your own behaviour gives a good model to copy for a child to learn how to behave.
5. Allow the child to make his own toy with whatever materials available (not to spend any amount on it). See the joy of the child. Definitely he will enjoy his creation more than the ones you purchase for him. Remember: Your comments should always convey appreciation. Most of the indoor games (like snake and ladder-board-dice-pawns included) the child can make by himself. He can make other toys of his requirements too.
6. Give a gadget to a child and watch what he learns from it and list it. Spend the same length of time with a child without any gadget, in a park, for example, and list what all you did together. Which one do you think is better?

7. When you teach a lesson to the child, bring out the possible real-life applications of it. The stories may be built up to bring the details of the lesson taught. Or it may be enacted. A child may be allowed to depict the lesson in his own drawings. This stays in the child's mind.
8. Whenever you move to punish a child by any kind of physical abuse, please stop yourself and think for a while, if the such action by your superior, what would be your reaction? Is it same or different? Why is it different when the doer is a child (or even wife)? You may imagine how you feel, when you are appreciated/ blasted by your superior for any small or big thing you did in your workplace. What motivates you and what pushes you back?
9. One must not act in anger. One must take a deep breath, leave the place, count from 100 to zero (if one is comfortable with numbers, otherwise from zero to 50), wash face with cold water, and drink a glass of cold water. Then ask oneself:

Will this incident make me angry tomorrow?

A week later?

A month later?

A year later?

Then issues fall into their place.

10. When children make you angry, think of Shri Ramakrishna's story of the snake. It is about hissing and not biting to kill. Observe your own anger. What does it indicate? Is it just a frustration or a helplessness expressing itself or anything else? What could be the

real reason behind it? By knowing your anger, you may know your child's anger too. (This technique was taught by a child to his friend.)

11. When a child behaves in any unwanted manner, please check for the model for such a behaviour. Surely there will be someone (it may be a television hero or a real known person, most of the times one of the parents) whom the child is imitating to get his wants. Check and correct that person or avoid exposure to events, simultaneously explaining to the child the bad things of his behaviour. He may pick up these models via technology as well.

12. **How to be happy?** A four-year old who was always happy and bubbly, was once asked how he was always happy. The answer was very straight forward. He smiled and said, 'Do like this (wear a smile) and you will be happy!' You too may try this technique to realise the capability of a child. Recently the Dalai Lama addressed school children and advised them to always smile when they meet people.

9

Play: Missing in Action in the Lives of Children

A BRIEF note on what play does for children. These have been scientifically proven.

Play is Universal Activity affecting all Development Domains

- Physical
- Intellectual
- Language
- Emotional
- Social
- Sexual
- Moral

Motor Development (Physical)

- Fine motor
- Gross motor

- Visuo-motor coordination
- Kinesthetic
- Tactile
- Complex movement of performing arts

Cognitive Domain (Intellectual)

- Attention
- Memory
- Problem solving
- Analysis and synthesis
- Planning steps
- Planning ahead

Language

- Expression of thoughts
- Communication with others
- Using written and spoken forms for communication
- Enhancing vocabulary

Social and Moral

- Cooperation
- Pro-social skills
- Following social rules: waiting for turn
- Following social rules of not cheating
- Leadership skills
- Power play
- Mastery play
- Innovative play
- Kinship play
- Therapeutic play

Emotional Domain

- Play releases tensions and pent-up emotions
- Play allows for compensation for loss, hurt or failures in fantasy

- Play facilitates self-discovery of most adaptive behaviour
- Play promotes awareness of conflicts revealed only symbolically or through displacement
- Play offers opportunity to re-educate children
- Play alters behaviour through role-play and story-telling
- Play is a medium of expression, learning, relationship and catharsis. Additional aspects of play consist of practicing and trying out new forms of behaviour which enhance creativity rather than adaptation

Parents come to Child Guidance Centres with complaints such as these:

The mother brings a five-year-old with the complaint,'My child wants to play all the time. He does not want to study!' with the firm belief that I will support her.

I ask her,'If children should not play–who else should?'

'But he does not want even to study.'

'Why should he? Is it fun?'

'No. But he should grow up to become a doctor. That is why.'

'Does he want to?'

'No. But we want him to.'

You would think this is an uncommon event. But we see it all the time. The parents wanting a two-year-old, three-year-old, four-year-old or a five-year-old to give up play and study.

In their own childhood they themselves were not deprived of play.

The teachers too share this opinion. They too believe that children should not play and study all the time.

On the other hand, the child naturally wonders why he is denied play. Between the school and home, the child's world consists of studies and more studies that consists of mostly rote learning. *The fun of learning that each child is entitled to is denied him/her, both at home and school.*

Both the teachers and parents worship a demon called 'The Syllabus'. In fact, syllabus is the goal and end product if preceded with joyful learning and is attained automatically. If the child enjoys reading from first grade, no text book is hard. If the focus is shifted from rote learning to real learning (comprehension), the books become meaningful and easy. It is the means and – not the end. Joyless, dreary rote learning is the result of mindless worship of syllabus. The goal should be to make the child an empowered learner who loves to learn. No child should be deprived of play and joyful learning.

Though play is a universal activity of childhood, Indian parents and teachers view it as a purposeless and useless activity.

However, it is one of the firmly established principles of psychology that play is very essential for the child's development process. Through play, children develop their intellectual, emotional, perceptual, motor and social skills. If one looks at any of the games played by children in India, one would be astounded by the abilities required in playing marbles or hopscotch, or the sensori-motor skills and geometry required to execute the traditional art of drawing *rangoli* or *kolam* (decorative line drawings) in front of the house in South India.

The Dying Concept of Free Play

Free play seems to be a thing of the past! Children in our contemporary times have little or no time for free play, for exploring stuff and just playing what they like! Their time is mediated and orchestrated by hypercompetitive parents who push them from one activity to the other. My neighbour's child, all of six, is shunted from swimming camps to abacus classes to even a coaching for kids camp! Where do children have time to understand and explore their own passions? Are we so selfish that we want children to just be extension of our selves and probably fulfil our unfulfilled wishes?

Looking back, mine was a glorious childhood. My family just let me be and do what I liked. I was never forced into any activity. My grandfather surrounded me with story books and comics and I was reading from the age of four. No one told me 'you must read!' I read what I wanted and whenever I wanted. Sometimes I took up my crayons and coloured or just doodled. I would show these to the family and they would tell me what I could do better. No unnecessary praise, no pushing or goading! I also played around with Lego and built parks and put swings and slides. My grandfather showed me how machines work and I used to be thrilled at the switchboard and lights. Being a chemistry professor, he also showed me how to grow beautiful copper sulphate crystals in test tubes. It was not like formal science, but I really loved it and spent hours tinkering around with his stuff. No one came and told me,'you are wasting time!'

I was allowed to play outdoors as much as I wanted. There was no curfew on play hours except that I had to come home for milk and a snack and make sure I was not over exhausted. My grandmother had a playschool and so our garden space had a slide, seesaw and a swing. We had a huge *honge* tree and the swing was like a hammock. My aunt and I spent many afternoons sleeping here or reading Enid Blyton. We often played like Secret Seven or Famous Five, and pretended that we were sleuthing for something!

My evenings were spent on the streets with the other kids. We played cricket, catch-catch with a ball, chor-police, hide and seek, hopscotch and lagori. We always parked our bicycles outside and made sure we cycled in groups every day! Those days the streets had little traffic and it was absolutely safe to cycle. We would cycle from our home. It was exhilarating to cycle downhill with the wind in our hair and clothes!

Some days, the boys in our neighbourhood got out tires and we spent hours chasing these things with a stick! My friends would come home to play in our sandpit. We had plastic spades and little buckets. We added water to the sand and pretended to bake cakes. My grandmother would give us Cadbury gems to decorate our mud pies and cakes (which we actually ate). My hair and even my ears would have sand, but it was such fun! My mother never told me not to play in the mud or get my clothes dirty. In fact, I was encouraged to play in the mud, so I would get immunity.

When I look back, I know I learned so much from these games and free play. All of us kids learned cooperation and collaboration through our games. We learned science concepts through our play like when we would ask my grandfather why we needed so much energy to cycle uphill. None of us were mollycoddled or overprotected. If we had a fall and bled, it was okay. We would get cleaned up with Dettol and back again on the streets. If we cycled out too far, it was okay so long as we knew the way to get back home. If we went home with totally muddied clothes, it was okay so long as we showered.

I am sorry for the generations which are glued to their stupid screens (mobile, television and video games) and missing out on the real fun and learning in free play and games.

—Contributed by Namitha Kumar

Yet another experiment by the author between 2014 and 2016 with 15-session packages using the top down method English and Kannada graded story books have resulted in good reading skills in both the languages in children admitted under the RTE and urban government primary schools.

To conclude, child-centred play-way method can bring about changes in the education system aimed for and already achieved elsewhere in the developed world.

Whose Right to Education is it Any Way?

Recognising the disparity in the education provided by private and government schools, the Government of India promulgated the Right to Education Act (2009). Under this provision, the private as well as non-minority schools are required to give admission to 25 per cent of their available seats at preschool and primary school levels to children from disadvantaged homes and government schools. The managements, teachers and parents of the private schools resent this because of their mindsets for the following reasons:

1. These children from poor socio-economic status and cannot mix with their children as they lack in social skills.
2. Those admitted under the RTE lack age/class appropriate academic skills.
3. What is not mentioned is the loss of profit caused by these children despite some reimbursement by the State governments.

Because of the above reasons, these children are discriminated against in several devious, even in vicious ways. For example, they are kept in a separate room lacking in basic facilities, taught separately by a helper or a regional language teacher, humiliated by different nickname, wrist bands identifying them as RTE admission, not permitted to use sports and other extracurricular facilities to say the least. In essence, the so-called privileged adults and children lack social conscienceness!

The Right to Education (RTE) Act (2009) is a bold policy move in the right direction, despite the enormous problems encountered in its translation into reality. The reasons for these failures theoretically, logistically, economically and programmatically have been discussed thread bare by the experts, media and the lay public alike. We introduce an innovative solution to the so-far neglected yet crucial problem of how to make the 'misfit' children fit into the so called good school. Admission to good school alone is not a solution. As long as we do not offer satisfactory solution to this question, there will be acrimonious debates on the non-feasibility of implementation on a large-scale across the nation. An experiential account of empowering the children admitted under the provision of RTE, to make a seamless and confident entry into a new socio-economic and cultural school milieu through a bridge programme is included in the book.

It is to be expected that these first-graders from regional medium schools and mostly low literate backgrounds will experience difficulties in adjusting to the new social and learning circumstances effectively.

The aim was to provide free intervention programme to make the transition smooth, especially in their early days of the school. It also aimed at enhancing psycho-social development, reading, writing and mathematical skills and promoting creativity. The programme uses play, art, craft, games, number and language games, singing, dancing, music, drama, and so on. The programme relies entirely on play-way method and completely child-centred, hence requiring very little help from adults.

The accompanying adults, teacher's assistants or teachers are informally trained in the play way methods. This enables the participating school to start their own play way group while starting with the new batch of children in the coming years.

Misconception about Children that can be Remedied:

- Child is considered a misfit and is to be made to fit!

A Misfit as he/she lacks:

- Pre-requisite

- Academic Skills (3 'R's)
- Spoken English
- Socialisation
- Ability to Adjust, Play, Interact
- Use of Facilities like Toilet
- Cleanliness (Self/Clothes)

Six programmes were conducted between April 2014 and June 2017, a total of 171 children were provided intervention lasting 2 to 3 hours for two weeks in small groups. Most of them were admitted to class 1, but there were many from earlier batches in classes 2-5 as well who had made no progress earlier in the same so-called good school.

Child-centred play-way approach was used and no formal instructions were given.

Outcome evaluation with pre-and post-psychological assessment:

- Pre-academic skills – language and maths
- Attention
- Intelligence
- Self esteem

They showed marked improvement in Attention, Concentration and Intelligence. Most important improvement in enhanced self esteem of these children and in English and Kannada reading and number work. The teachers found these children adjusting well to class 1, consisting of the regular students. Teachers found they could not make out who were the RTE admissions, much to their surprise! In one school, which had 38 children in two batches, the children in the Bridge programme were found to be so lively and so involved, so much so, other parents and children were asking, who gave them tuitions? All the children in the Bridge programme were admitted to the best schools in Bangalore.

Bridge Programme for Children admitted Under RTE

Sustainability

- Teachers in the schools to be trained to carry forward the two-week package in the beginning of the year
- Workshop for teachers with lecture demonstration in schools
- There can be many more innovative models
- Observation of the play-way method promotes interest in the children as good learners

Self Esteem and Empowerment

- Improvement on cognitive functions and academic skills.
- Enhancement of self esteem occurs spontaneously as revealed in behaviours, language use for communication and pro-social skills.
- Observed ease of the empowered children on academics and social parameters upon entry into the regular classroom.

The Bridge programme was successful in its endeavour. It covered a total of 171 children. However, the demonstrable and dramatic success needs to be sustained by the schools. If a few teachers have hands on experience of child-centred play way methods, they can effectively provide intervention to each year's new RTE admissions before the opening of the school in summer.

Play is the most essential part of growing up. I would include it in the fundamental right of a child. Play is not a purposeless activity. It is the most essential ingredient of healthy overall development.

Let children play!

PART III
CHILDREN AND SOCIETY

10

Exploitation of the Child

SOCIETY AND individual family concerns are some of the issues that may not be attributed to anyone in particular. These vary in different societies. The examples are:

- Child of a single parent (more often the mother)
- A child of divorced parents
- An adopted child
- Child in an orphanage/remand home
- Children of HIV infected, alcohol dependent, psychotic or criminal parents
- Homeless and runaway children
- Natural and man-made disasters may produce large scale distress and place children at high risk as the protective fabric of the family and society of the child is destroyed

All the above children are at risk if they lack support from the family and are recipients of adverse reactions from society.

Common problems can be circumvented if there is a supportive extended family, which will provide care for the children even under dire circumstances and warm and unconditional love. In India, the grandparents, uncles and aunts most willingly help out. This is a characteristic of a traditional society like India where there is extensive bonding. For example, relatives do take care of orphaned children in the best manner possible. A single mother or a working mother is helped greatly by the grandparents on the paternal or maternal side.

Children of divorce have problems of divided loyalties and are often torn apart and insecure emotionally. Legal problems create very unpleasant environment for children.

Adoption is often discouraged by Indian society unless it is within family. Adopted children have distinct stresses due to societal attitudes.

Who Are My Parents?

Sanjay, a fourteen-year-old, ran away from home after being reprimanded about his poor academic performance. On talking with the parents, we came to know that their only child was adopted and was never told about it. A few months ago, while the family was attending a get-together, a relative had remarked to the mother, 'Is this the boy whom you adopted? He looks so much like his father'. The mother changed the subject and never talked about it with her son even after that.

Parents' Dilemma

a. Revealing the truth to the child

What is the consequence if revealing that the child is adopted does not happen at an early stage of the child? When it does not happen at the right time and children have heard it from others, they have felt betrayed and the very foundation of a lovingly nurtured parent-child relationship collapses. It is said, to start 'telling' the child should happen from day one. Is the child able to understand is the question. It is not for the 'child' but for the parents to be comfortable with the term 'adoption'. This will help the parents to talk about it with the 'child' before he/she comes to know of it from others. Every child adopted needs to know about his/her history. In some adoptive families, the child may even strongly resemble the adopted parents. So, the parents feel that 'nobody will be able to make out'. Some parents are not comfortable with telling the child and prefer to say that they have forgotten that the child was adopted.

b. To inform the school or not

Parents of a six-year-old child were taken by surprise to find a column in the admission form asking if the child was adopted. But they would not like all the teachers to know. The reason, they may start treating the child differently. The teachers may label the child or expectations may become low. More so, the child may be judged as 'because he/she is adopted'.

On the contrary, there are good reasons to keep the school informed. Parents prefer the school to learn about adoption from them directly rather than through somebody who will not be sensitive to the word 'adoption'.

> A parent reported that the subject of 'adoption' was dealt with in her daughter's class in a very insensitive manner. The topic 'family' was being discussed in class IV and children were asked to get their family photograph and theirs, when they were a month old. When an adopted girl went and told the teacher about the non-availability of her family photograph, the immediate response of the insensitive teacher was,'how will you have it when you have bad blood in you'. The girl started hating that subject and the teacher. When we use

insensitive language to talk about the child's history, it hurts a child to the very core.

Adoption is an alternative way of extending one's family. It is accepting a child which is not yours as your own and bringing into one's family. Our Indian epics honour the concept of adoption; grandparents tell their grand children stories about Krishna, Karna, Shakuntala. Adoption was no secret in those days, neither a stigma nor a taboo. We need to think and speak positively about the three stakeholders involved in the adoption circle: Birth Parents, Adoptive Parents and the child.

—*Contributed by Sheela Kamath*

Institutionalised children are at risk of physical and psychological abuse. The staff of the institution are often low paid, untrained and have little inclination to be supportive to children. In the government-run institutions, there is lack of motivation to help children and the supervision of undesirable staff activities are lacking. In privately run institutions, there is even more scope for physical and sexual abuse from the higher-level functionaries. These could be religious charitable institutions and otherwise. The newspapers are replete with examples of such abuse. The children not only lack emotional support but are threatened constantly by antisocial functionaries.

The above are only a tip of the iceberg, where children are exposed to psychological and physical abuse by society. However, these cannot be blamed entirely on society because it is morally corrupt individuals who harm the helpless children under their care.

Deliberate exploitation by adults for profit to the adults is visible and tangible. These have been covered in detailed manner by various Acts of the Children Protection Bill POCSO.

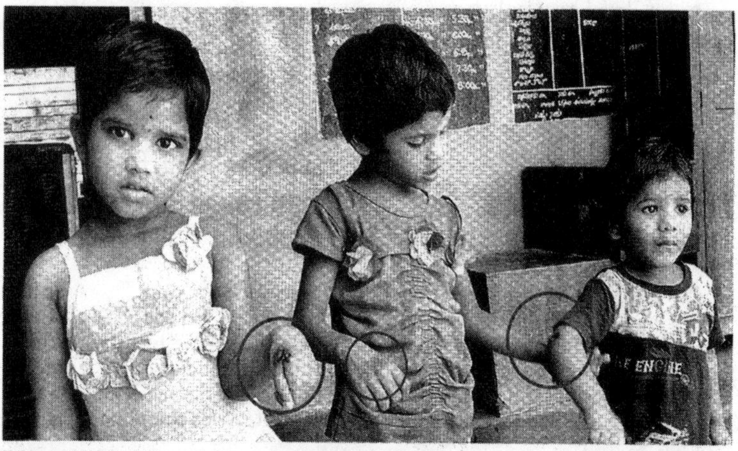

Children of Shishu Griha, a state-run orphanage in Karimnagar, showing burn marks on their arms

Caretakers Brand Seven Kids at Karimnagar Orphanage

by Naveen Kumar Tallam

Karimnagar: In a shocker, two women caretakers at Shishu Griha, a state-run orphanage in Karimnagar district of Telangana, mercilessly tortured a group of children by branding their tender hands with scalding hot spoons for not eating food served to them.

The punishment left the children, all below five years of age, with blisters on their hands.

The horrifying incident, though occurred on Friday, came to light on Tuesday night after video footage of the torture surfaced. Following instructions from Karimnagar district Collector Neetu Prasad, criminal cases have been registered against the two caretakers, who are at large. Orders were issued to remove another caretaker from service.

The seven infants, including a two-year-old boy, were tortured on Friday as they didn't consume the food served to them. A caretaker Buchamma picked up a service spoon, heated it by directly holding it over the gas flame.

Buchamma then handed over the heated spoon to another caretaker Padma, who used it to brand the wrist of a child.

But she did not stop at that. Padma injured three other children sitting near her. The helpless children squirmed, withdrew and hid their injured hands in the back as a reflex.

But the horror did not stop as Padma stood up and injured three more kids, while Buchamma watched amusingly - as seen in the CCTV footage.

The Shishu Griha at Mankammathota in Karimnagar is managed by the Women and Child Welfare Department. About eight children, all below five-years age and orphans, were admitted at the Shishu Griha for rehabilitation.

- Child trafficking
- Child pornography
- Child prostitution
- Child labour – in the factories and as domestic servants
- Kidnapping (selling of children, giving for adoption and abusive homes)
- Using children for begging by gangs
- Child marriages

These usually are networks of adults who share the profits with the police and other profit-making network of services. Once again, these have been documented extensively yet the menace continues.

There are documented research highlighting the purchase of pretty lambani girl children from the poor parents, often offering adoption and schooling. The offers are actually entirely motivated by profiteering and traffic of these young girls.

Durga was a nine-year-old who was brought to our child psychiatric services by the nuns. She was found by the police who witnessed her being abused by some men in the railway station. She was placed in a convent orphanage. She was indulging in overtly sexual behaviour with other girls. The convent staff was appalled by this behaviour. When she was brought, no one knew anything about her. I used the play-way method to reach out her. During the play sessions, she enacted many of the traumatic events in her sad life. At times she showed what happened to her in action and at times by repeating the entire conversations over several sessions. The following story emerged.

Theirs was a very poor family and she had a younger brother. Her parents loved the brother. In fact, they sold her to some men who brought her to Bangalore. They brought her clothes and gifts and sexually abused her. She repeated sexual conversations with display of guilt. For example, 'Cover yourself, don't display your body' and so on. As she revealed the source of her distress, her misbehaviour in the orphanage disappeared entirely and she started showing interest in going to the school for the first time. It shows, children who are sexually abused tend to repeat the same behaviour but can be helped to come out of the trauma if they are able to express these to a sympathetic and non-judgemental counsellor.

When children are caught in the web of deception by adults who use them as objects to be bought and sold, who is going to stand up to them to protect the children? We should all emulate Kailash Sathyarthi in protecting our children-at-risk in our own small ways.

It is not society as a whole but a few individuals creating a network of deception. *But why are there not many who can take up the cause on behalf of society? Why are we the silent majority? Why do the police overlook or at times even profit from these crimes? Why are we the bystanders to the cruelty to children in public places?*

It is to be noted that legally, there are recourses to solve every kind of exploitation mentioned above. But can young children stand up and fight? We need many socially committed groups to fight these evil networks on behalf of children. We need more Kailash Sathyarthis in our country.

While legal protection can be sought, it is the social conscience that we need to worry about. The kind of tortures these children undergo, do we stand and watch passively if they were to be our children?

There is so much anger when prices of petrol, vegetables and pulses go up. There is so much of anger when our salaries are not hiked. We go on strikes. We show our anger towards the government officials or politicians promoted very actively by the visual and social media. *Is justifiable anger reserved only for adult causes? (Mainly finance-related ones!)*

Why do we as a country fail our children? There is huge hue and cry when someone is molested, raped or killed in careless accidents. These are individual acts of violence. *But why do we fail to recognise the mass violence against children?*

The Juvenile Justice Act and the Protection of Children from Sexual Offences Act (POCSO) are there to protect these children. But we should make use of them. For example, any person who witnesses abuse, sexual or otherwise is obliged to report it to the right authority. There is helpline for assistance as well.

Perhaps we need to identify these groups of victims and perpetrators and have a watchdog with conscience to monitor these trouble spots.

Steps Involved

- Social awareness that something wrong is happening with victims
- Name, shame and fire or jail the perpetrators
- Offer sensible solutions to prevent future such occurrences
- Destroy the privileges of these networks

It is possible to eliminate these evil forces in society. One could start it in a small way in a village or a small town and then spread the awareness across the nation. These programmes need to be taken on public health prevention model.

To summarise, there are individuals who are basically cruel and uncaring, who find it lucrative to exploit young children. They get sadistic joy, their greed being satisfied with minimal effort as it is easy to manipulate and traffic children as they are weak, small and lured easily by devious means. These people, I consider to be the most evil among human beings.

11

Exploitation across Caste, Class and Ethnicity

IN THIS chapter, we discuss the problems faced by children across our society which is a general form of exploitation based on misguided views of society. In addition, there are groups of children who are exposed to negligence of physical and psychological nature because of who they are.

Class and Caste Differences: In earlier times, castes determined one's social standing. In a feudal system, the Brahmins were at the top with the Shudras at the bottom of the hierarchy. Subsequent to these four-fold division, an inextricable web of subcategories evolved, each claimed superiority over the other. With the affirmative action of reservation for lower castes, came up the greed of exploiting the benefits offered to the lower castes. This led to the reversal of the demand for lower class. We want the benefits of affirmative action, though we are not really of lower class. So came the demand for high caste reservation policy. It involves a paradox of people with social advantage who deny the privileges they have to those who do not have it. Whatever is the psychology of reservation, the castes remain away from each other. The caste discrimination occurs at all levels.

The Dalit parents and children continue to suffer social disadvantage. What have the children done to suffer the same fate in the safety net of schools? The teachers, who are of higher caste, truly believe that 'untouchables are unteachable'. The fact is that these children, whose parents are illiterate, have little access to books or magazines at their homes. They hold pencils in their hands for the first time when they join the school. They have no access to toys of the kind other children have. But that does not make them unteachable. They all are intelligent and creative as any other child.

If only the teachers knew how to bring it out and make the child an empowered child. Upper class (caste) teachers and children discriminate against those whom they consider socially inferior. Despite literacy and wealth, people continue to be caste ridden in India. Inter caste eating together, lower caste people entering temples are still taboos in the mindsets of most people. *The only silver lining is the provision by the Sarva Shiksha Abhiyan of midday meals in all government schools. The single provision has paid dividends in terms of social harmony.*

Don't We Have Rights? A Dalit Story

It was a family with parents and three children: a boy and two girls. They were living in a village. The parents were working for the village head – father in his fields and mother at his house and fields. They were living happily, in spite of their poverty.

The children went to a school which was quite far from their home and village. They wanted to study well and were good at their studies. Parents too wished to give them a good education. They didn't involve the children in to their hard labours. The eldest one, the boy, finished his 10th standard. Parents wanted to send him to college. But where was the money to do so? Father went to ask his owner for the money. He reluctantly agreed to give only a part of it. The father was content with it and left with a hope to get the remaining when actually needed. The boy was admitted to a college, in a city, accommodated in a free hostel. The boy studied well and scored well.

The mother fell sick after some months. They were left with no money to treat her. It worsened day-by-day and finally she succumbed to it. The father was trying to take care of the two daughters. They too took care of the house-hold, along with their studies. Seeing their mother suffer without any medical help, they had decided to become doctors and help people like them in the village.

In the meantime, the owner began pestering the father for returning his loan. He pleaded to get some more time to return the amount. But the owner did not agree to it. Helplessly, the father committed suicide.

The elder boy returned to the village for good, burying all his ambitions of studying along with his father's body. He took charge of the household. He determined to see that his sisters continued their studies. He began working for the same owner for his livelihood. Along with that, he began working as an electrician for his and neighbouring villagers. He earned more than his father did. The family was moving smoothly. His sisters scored high in their deciding exams and successfully entered medical college. They studied without any hurdle, as they got scholarships. They became doctors.

They returned to their village to set up a clinic. They did not have that much money. Their brother met with an accident and did not survive, in spite of their serious efforts. They were bold enough to take care of themselves. They went to their father's owner to get some loan to set up a clinic, their life's ambition. He in turn wanted them to share his bed before parting with any amount. Shocked, they tried to convince him not to behave in that manner. He was adamant.

They felt totally defeated and returned home, utterly helpless. Ultimately, they followed their father's footsteps and ended their lives.

The above is a story narrated by a girl from a Girijana School in Karnataka. It sounded filmy and she was asked for its source. She said it was a story told by her granny who witnessed it happening in her place.

—Contributed by Rajalakshmi

Gender Discrimination

Gender discrimination is all-pervasive in society. Indian society in general is patriarchal. There are exceptions in the west coast and north east of matrilineal system of inheritance. While legally gender discrimination is not permissible, it is still practised widely. Starting from female infanticide leading to skewed gender ratio across the country and the other indicators, preferential treatment of boys is widely seen across all sections of society—especially in access to better health care, schooling etc. However, the provision of free education to all has brought about a major difference in the lives of girls. Now girls do go to school in large numbers.

Gender discrimination is much reduced as the size of the family has shrunk. When most families have one child or two children, fair play is evident across gender. Some anomalous practices in the society do correct themselves over a period of time. There are several reports of better school performance by girls when compared to the boys.

Disabilities

Disabilities such as orthopedic, intellectual, visual and hearing disabilities put children under risk, especially with regards to school admission and absence of support measures at school. In most of the urban areas in India, there are special schools of excellent, mediocre and poor kids available to children with disabilities. Unfortunately, these special schools segregate them from normal school children and thus deprive them of exposure to normal and healthy interactions with peers and teachers. In the rural areas, families and schools are far more tolerant of disabled children. These children can obtain assistance and disability appliances and aids. However, it is not easy for villages to apply for such facilities. However, an Anganwadi worker, health worker or a primary health care doctor can help them by facilitating the process of application. Disabled children may lack in one aspect of their pre-social domain but they too deserve environment that they can share with all the other children. But other children too need to learn not to discriminate and deal with them ethically and support them.

Inner Experiences of Children with Disabilities

Children with disabilities/disorders can have either of the two experiences: excessive mollycoddling or indifference from parents and caregivers. This case will illustrate the first of the kind.

> Savita was just 6 years and the youngest child. Her two elder siblings were normal kids and it turned out that Savita had Thalassemia.
>
> Her parents were naturally worried about her health and progress, but they went too far in being so protective that they literally smothered all her natural interests. She was not allowed to play with other kids for fear of infections. She was not allowed to go outside and play because she might fall and bleed. She played at home with 1-2 kids who were kind enough to keep her company and play board games. She was carefully watched over by her older siblings and parents. If she showed the slightest sign of tiredness, she would be immediately taken to the hospital for blood tests, necessary or not! She was also closely monitored in school by teachers who had been instructed by the parents. She could never take

part in the activities that she wanted to. Sports were barred for her altogether. Though the doctors advised the parents time and again to let her take part in physical activities, they just kept her indoors most of the time.

Savita grew up to be a fearful kid because she was programmed to believe that she was delicate and not capable of doing things which others normally did. There are several kids who have the same disorder who do everything from swimming to trekking. Yet, Savita was excluded from all activities. She believed danger lurked in every corner and something fatal might happen to her. She did not believe in herself and did not have the self-confidence to venture out on her own anywhere. She became dependent on her parents and siblings even when it came to decisions like choosing an academic course. Her own identity was blurred because she was so overshadowed by others. She didn't know who she was and what she wanted out of life because she was used to others doing everything for her.

Savita is a grown-up young lady today but just as risk-averse, frightened and unsure. She has lost the compass of life and doesn't know where she is going. If Savita has to go ahead in life she has to come out of the shadow of fear and uncertainties which plague her constantly.

—*Contributed by Namitha Kumar*

Mainstreaming such special children in normal schools is considered to be the right option. Yet the schools need to develop sensitivities and supports for these children. This needs lot of preparation on the parts of teachers and other children. But in the long run, it demands teacher's compassion,which is a much-desired value in a healthy society.

In the rural areas, there are no extra provisions for disabled children. Mainstreaming occurs automatically as they are admitted to the closest primary school. In general, there seem to be more pro-social behaviour evident in the rural schools.

But the issue of providing additional support to the disabled remains a difficult problem. It is true that the Ministry of Social Justice provides enormous amounts of funding towards the welfare of the disabled. In addition, there are equally large number of non-governmental and charity organisations catering to the needs of the disabled from childhood to adulthood. The physical and psychological needs are different and we need a nuanced approach to alleviate their distress.

It may seem that the class/caste discrimination mainly affect the 'Dalits' adversely in two ways because of the mindset of the rest.

a. Because they belong to a lower strata they deserve to be where they are.
b. If 'they' are given special benefits they are depriving 'us' from what we so rightly deserve.

These two false beliefs drive harsh and cruel treatments leading to bitterness. The gender discrimination probably will gradually fade away, once equality is upheld legally as women are capable of uplifting themselves on their own merits. Someday, society may also become sensitive to disabilities and may veer around to adopting healthier attitude towards them.

Discrimination based on religions has a tendency to lead to polarisation of different communities. This is the worst-case scenario in terms of social harmony, for children and adults alike.

Unfortunately, political parties initiate, maintain and exploit the democratic secular fabric of this country for their own selfish gains, using each of the above mentioned conflicted situations. This is a manmade disaster in addition to the several due to natural faultlines.

12

Exploitation of Children through Marketing

IN THIS chapter, two aspects will be focused upon. One is about impact of advertisements on children. The other is the use of the child as a commodity.

Awareness Programmes and Advertisements

Children are being widely used in advertising and what are the psychological aspects that companies look for when depicting children in their advertisements needs to be examined.

There are two ways in which advertisement can psychologically affect children. These could be for the benefit of the children as seen in the promotional activities such as polio eradication, immunisations and in general, maternal and child nutrition, AIDs, drugs/alcohol and smoking awareness and many such preventive medicine community efforts. These may be termed awareness programmes and meant only for the public good.

There is another category which is subversive and devious in the style of communication and touches the so-called baser emotions of the children and the adults around them. We shall describe marketing endeavours under TRAP (Television, Radio and Print media). These are **one-way** media. In chapter 13, we shall explore the impact of two-way media.

1. Ads for Baby Foods, Growth Enhancing Tonics

Some examples are: Paediatricians do not recommend supplements instead of normal home cooked food. They don't recommend biscuits, chocolates, savoury eatables and what comes under 'junk food' category. Nor do they recommend so called tonics for physical growth and brain development. But advertisements are replete with examples promoting these unhealthy trends, using children as models. At times portraying them as superman or superwoman!

Aerated and high calorie drinks, sweets make the child want to have it when watching the commercial advertisements. The advertisements may target children directly in the present, or in the future in adulthood themselves, or these may give children the power to pester their parents to buy for them or parents themselves buy of desire (toys to luxury cars/television etc).

Advertising affects children in different ways. Their age, experience and how much of what they see is discussed with those around. Young children understand advertisements differently at different ages.

At 0–2 years, the child cannot tell the difference between advertisements and actual programmes.

At 3–6 years, the child can differentiate advertisements from programmes but they do not understand that these advertisements are trying to sell something. They find them helpful and entertaining. They are not critical of the claims, such as taking a particular tonic will make him a superman!

7–11 years, the primary school child can understand that the advertisements are trying to sell something and narrate key aspects such as the jingles they hear. But they do not understand the products may not be as good or that the bad points are not described.

You can limit the viewing of commercials directly or through applications. Most importantly, you can discuss the commercials your child is comfortable with, and ask the child following questions:

1. What is the product being advertised?
2. What is it for?
3. Who is it for?

With an older child you can ask, what are the plays used in the advertisements such as use of celebrities to promote a product, does it make them more grown up, stronger or better looking if they use the product and does it give you something free when you buy the product?

Some common advertising gimmicks.

- Bribe (free gift)
- The game
- Big claims and promises
- Super person in making
- Cartoon character you like
- Special photography effect to make the product attractive
- Repetition (reinforces the effect)
- Music (attractive jingles)

All the above are psychological principles used in persuading suggestible young mind.

Consumer Goods of Daily Use

The children are made to sell objects of daily use, be it tooth paste, soap, insurance and children are portrayed as grownups and adults as simple and childish! Is it to demonstrate to the children that they have better judgments than the adults around them? This makes them entitled to control adults.

Products are sold through ads that are sponsored by the manufacturers, which hold reality shows and competitions for the children.

There are even more devious ploys to promote acquisition of objects of desire. Theses show children and adults indulging in anti-social and amoral behaviours. Examples abound but to list a few: the child indulges in deception while talking on a mobile to the parents, the child wants a bigger and showy car, child/adult brags about a grand car or an HD television set and other children are made to feel jealous of the ownership of such an object. Those who own ordinary televisions are mocked at by children. The advertisements promote a highly materialistic and selfish culture. Sometimes children are used to make fun of adults, to induce them to act as grown ups.

Unfortunately, even adults fall prey to the devious marketing strategies. The ability to judge what is good for us is diminished. We jump to the conclusion that whatever is portrayed is really good! If we have no discretion, how do we expect our children not to fall for these devious means?

An exercise: Prepare a list of all the consumables you buy for a month and see how much is decided by advertisements and how much on your experience of the product.

As a child psychologist, I ask a question: *Are there no ethical guidelines when it comes to exploitation of children through advertisements?*

Perhaps it should come under Child Labour and Regulation Act. Physical damage can be measured while psychological damage is immeasurable. Should we as responsible adults not protect our children?

2. Use of Children as Commodities

Exploitation of Children through Reality Shows

A fine line exists between promoting talent and exploiting it by the parents, media and the producers of the shows. But the misery of those who lose can only be imagined by us. The winners are expected to dress, talk, dance in overtly seductive and sexualised manner, as adults do. One wonders about the sanity of those adults around the child who cause this loss of innocence and deprivation of childhood itself.

The Pros and Cons of Promotion of Talent:

- A child has talent and is very gifted. He may have a dedicated teacher who is not bothered about publicity but only wishes to enhance the child's talent. Publicity means extending the fame for the mentor, parent or the promoter. The gifted child is a cash cow.
- Every child is entitled to healthy overall development at home, school and a finally a 'job'. Normal home life and school life should be the norm when they are growing up. How does one differentiate 'stardom' from 'child labour' in young children?
- The child is pushed from a single goal of singing to multiple goals of singing all kinds of music and all kinds of dancing (include Bollywood item dancing!). Yes, it does look cute when a 4-year-old seductively dances. Does, anyone think, what is the child's understanding of the meaning and of the content of the lyrics and body language? In addition, to dress young children

in 'seductive clothing' and introduce adult dancers on whose bodies the young ones carry out dance gymnastics! With so much of body contact with strangers – what is its impact on the growing child's awareness? I have seen mothers applying heavy makeup on very young girls. Where does childhood end and adolescence with awakened sexuality begin?

- Sometimes even advertisement eliciting attractive feelings in order to draw donation for a charity cause may use pictures of a slum child or a disfigured child; they too use the child as a commodity to sell an idea.

3. Schools run as Profit-making Industries

Historically in the colonial times, good schools were run by missionaries. Some with the motive of converting the local heathen (non-Christians), some of course with truly altruistic motives.

After independence, the Government of India extended the school system to cover the entire nation to provide mass education. In the earlier times, schools were run by teachers who believed that teaching was a noble profession. Unfortunately, later on it became like any other job. While the private schools or the so-called convent schools mushroomed with good facilities and high free structure, eventually this became a money spinning industry promoted by excellent marketing strategies.

Now we are left with the elitist and expensive schooling with English as the medium of instruction and government schools providing, as reported by ASER and NCERT, poor quality education with the medium being regional languages. Regional language offers rootedness to one's own culture while English medium promotes connectivity across India and the world and most importantly paves the way to upward social mobility. *Our aim should be to provide quality mass education both in English and the regional language.* My own experience shows that this is desirable and definitely possible.

When one observes advertisements in visual media, posters and other promotional efforts, education seems to have become a saleable good. How to make your child a leader, a topper in the class. Excellent facilities offered makes that school the most desirable one. Similar marketing efforts go on for coaching classes and tuitions as well. The aim is to fleece the parents. When did education become a commodity to be sold and bought?

4. Special Classes (Tuition and Coaching Classes)

Apart from the above, numerous advertisements offer classes in dance, music, art, gymnastics, yoga, ABACUS, Spoken English, drama and so on. The important question is what is the profit margin of these enterprises? Do children need so many activities? Did the parents themselves have so many activities in their childhood? Who wants them? Children or the parents?

Some questions:

i. Are these essential?
ii. Does the child want it?
iii. How expensive is it and can the family afford it?
iv. Should the child not have time to play or even not do anything at all?
v. Will the child pursue it later on?

As long as the marketing aims at profit, it is less likely that benefit to the chid will be in focus. Where has the lofty ideal providing quality education for all children gone?

All the above TRAPS appear very innocuous and harmless because even adults fall prey to them. It is important parents themselves analyse the impact of advertisements (or even the seriously morally compromised soap operas on television) and determine how these impacts their own day to day behaviour. I end with one example. A child of ten years, who watched television for four hours in the absence of parents, was asked to write ten good points about the television as homework. He turned up with ten points—but all with negative aspects of television. If a ten-year-old can discriminate good and bad, can we not do the same?

13

Perilous Development from Reality to Virtual Reality

UNDER THIS chapter, we shall examine impact of visual media—Television, Radio and Print and Internet (Internet of Things, IoT as a catagory) and Artificial Intelligence (AI)—which are interactive. Both may impact children adversely. The focus in this chapter is on psychological impact on children at different ages.

Visual Media and Children

Studies appear to suggest viewing of violence on screen by children has adverse effect in terms of facilitating subsequent aggressive behaviour. However, those in the industry of media, ask an ingenious question: 'Would you become a serial murderer after seeing a movie on the theme?' Some suggest even of its cathartic value. Some believe that statistical significance probably of two per cent is not something to be concerned about. There are other more important contributors such as poverty, family violence etc. Thus, a definite suggestion predisposing personality traits and vulnerability, make some children more vulnerable and at risk. This controversy reflects a basic difference of predilection for environmental or genetic contributors. Thus, there are several nuanced positions one can take.

a. Only the vulnerable children along with non-supportive families and low socio-economic status and who extensively view television violence are likely to end up as criminals, while for the majority it is an innocuous or even an educative medium.

However, research trends have changed a good deal in the recent years.

The US Commission on Causes and Prevention of Violence in 1969 had stated that television was not a 'principal' cause but a contributing factor along with low income and unstable homes. The revised 1982 update has supported a closer positive relationship between television and violence.

b. Aggression is a learnt behaviour.

Longitudinal studies suggested a small effect, along with other predictors like environment on personality. The British and Finnish studies tend to support more environmental vantage view point. Experimental studies showed that violence is learnt through different ways through the visual media:

- Imitation
- Activating latent tendencies for aggression
- Desensitisation to sympathy for the victim
- Accept violence as normal way to conflict resolution

British television viewer violence and crime rates among adolescents are less than US television viewer violence and crime rates. Many of the retrospective studies suggest stronger links than earlier suspected. Studies linked violent crime, wife and child abuse across all socio-economic strata and IQ. There is a report that viewing of violent and pornographic videos was a significant causal factor for subsequent act.

c. In a dynamic approach to understanding of aggression, the role of television in the development of superego, replacing the family as the sole influencing agent before the advent of television has too been highlighted.

d. The developmentalists highlight stages of moral development where between the age of 1 and 4 years, there is self-centered morality; at 5 years, more acceptable morality; between 5 and 7 years, preoccupation with justice; and between 8-14 years concern that people should think well of them. Thus what the child views and understands depends on his/her stage of development. What comes over in television programmes may be understood quite differently by the child at different stages of development.

Based on field and clinical experience, psychodynamic and behavioural theories and most of all from a developmental perspective, the author takes the position that indiscriminate viewing of visual media, especially with violent content, interferes with normal development.

A child attains the normal development in the different domains such as physical, cognitive, language, emotional, social, moral and sexual development. These occur in specific unique fashion, in infancy, childhood (early, middle and late) and adolescence (early and late).

Any event is seen, understood and responded to differently by children at the different stages. On the other hand, most of the programmes are created by adults who presume to know the developmental levels of the children. The child goes through four stages of cognitive development and can understand the events limited by understanding of that particular stage.

It is thus essential that children need to be explained about the meaning of an event as meant to be conveyed. A child may completely misunderstand the message. This may apply even to popular books like the *Harry Potter* volumes. But very few of the very young can access it. However, visual media is open to all, no matter what age.

My own experience with children brought to a child guidance centre reveals the impact of indiscriminate television viewing. It shows that regardless of the age of the child, indiscriminate viewing has serious repercussions. These may manifest as poor interaction with the caretakers, and continuous looking at television in a four-month-old, fear reaction to violent scenes, where the mother had her nine-month-old on her lap, while viewing television.

Long-term social and emotional deprivation coupled with long hours of television viewing has been encountered in children present with autistic symptoms. Short-term manifestation of aggression, whining, temper tantrums and fear reaction soon after hours of television view too has been noted. In an interesting experience with 800 tribal primary school children, noted was the complete absence of aggression, hyperactivity and attention deficiency. In the 400 urban children, on the other hand, 10 were over active, one suffered from hyperkinetic syndrome.

In Indian Homes

- Adults and children share television viewing and very few of them are suitable for young children.
- Adults and children alike view television into late hours, thus depriving children of much needed sleep with longer exposure to television.
- Descriptive accounts of reduced interest in school work both in cities and rural areas have been found.
- Especially since the advent of video, cable and satellite technology, there is unlimited supply of unsuitable material in one's own home.

- Use of television instead of baby sitters.
- Viewing of television is encouraged instead of play. Play promotes the overall development of children, while television viewing does not.

Till two-and-a-half years, Vijay lived in an apartment, where majority of the flats were vacant. His mother was kept away from any outings or outdoor activities and had nobody to talk to. The first word he imitated was 'Soppu', picked up from what he had heard a street vendor shout, selling greens. This was the only sound he got to hear repeatedly every morning.

He now lives in a place where no other house welcomes anyone, nor do any of his neighbours enter his house, in spite of various and varied efforts. He, being a shy child, had very few people around him to interact with. Thus, he found /was exposed to television as the only companion other than his limited/restricted family members from a very young age, since when he was about three years old.

Evening was his TV time. His parents tried to be sensitive to what he watches. Initially, baby shows – with only flowers swinging/swaying, butterflies flying, fishes swimming, with a slow music, these were his shows. Very soon he got bored of them. He wanted a next level. Disney shows, which had only adventures, inventions, without any violence, of course, from an adult perspective, were put for him. Thus his shows went on an upgrading procedure on a regular basis.

I kept observing, what was going on with Vijay. He stopped going out for a walk in the evenings. He began to wait for the dusk fall, so that he gets his TV time. The waiting was gradually converted into a longing, an urge, and finally an addiction-like habit. It was an addiction, by the time he was four. And that was time specific.

The results were: once his television time was over, he was not the same child, Vijay, that he was prior to that time. He was irritable, crying, cranky, unable to understand whatever others did or said. I often wondered, 'Is this the same child as the one before his TV time?'

I kept thinking, when a child like him–an overly sensitive, sensible, mature, understanding, kind, empathetic child-- behaves this way after watching such, comparatively milder versions, of the cartoons or children's films, it shows, what would be the state of children with different temperaments…! What makes him so much disturbed? And what drags him to get into such a state again? He was ready to do anything, be anywhere, with anyone, even to stay alone at home, if he were allowed to be with the gadget and its free gifts. A child, with and without a gadget, was as if two entirely different persons.

This continued for nearly four years and more. I watched helplessly. Despite trying, I didn't achieve much. I had observed that my being in his school, though for ONLY TWO days, had made him look at me with a difference. I thought of reaping some benefit from this.

Recently, from April 2018, when Vijay turned 7, I decided to work with him. I began taking him to places of his choice, worked and spoke to make him work with his hands, whenever in Mysuru. I took him to a paper-cutting workshop (I too attended it with him).

Trains are his fascination. We had many train trips together. Then one day (22.05.2018) I took him to the Railway station. From purchasing the platform ticket, he was the one who had to direct me. He met and spoke to the station managers, engine drivers, some of the special passengers (The CRP force, returning from their election duty, to Delhi, to take care of Amarnath Pilgrims). He felt very happy with his railway station visit. That afternoon, after we returned home, he wanted to watch the trains again on the laptop and he convinced his grandfather to let him. After that, I spoke to him in detail. I asked him to compare his joy at seeing the train and its people, talking to them, to his watching trains on screen. He thought for some time. He was able to express his understanding of the events. It was, as always, a wonderful piece of explanation that came from him.

Then he decided that he has to come out of the 'Possession', a word he used for his addiction. This was on 22nd May, as stated earlier. He is working on getting away from television very seriously. He expresses his struggle to fight out that desire, possession, or *the witch*, who forces him to watch TV or reach for a laptop or mobile. And he controls himself and stays away from them.

I watch in amazement, the level of control this child is able to exercise and his potential. It has been a wonderful experience for me to follow Vijay's journey. I had brought him for your talk (Malavika Kapur's). Though he was busy with his train imitations and working with his seed collections, I am sure that he has absorbed many of the things, you (Malavika) said.

At the end of it, Vijay also observed, 'Amma has to stop watching TV and mobile, only then she can be a better Amma'.

A child is a fresh entry into this world and has to deal with various things, at different, multiple levels. It's a multi-dimensional (not just a three-dimensional) world captured, controlled, restricted into a two dimensional screen. This mars the viewing, distorts the actual, factual dimensions and confuses a child, at a very young age. Those designing Artificial Intelligence (AI) may join their hands with psychologists, paediatricians, and other significant people concerned with a child's developmental process and should together and in consultation decide the age or the stage for the first exposure of a child to visual technology. Then, the quality of the contents being telecast or provided on gadgets are to be decided by a national regulatory authority. Also these content need to pass a child-friendly design test. It is the responsibility of a parent to know what all the child watches on a screen. Even then, we as adults, view it from a totally different perspective when compared to a child. Today it is worrisome at all levels, and that makes every solution as an impossibility.

Debates in this area are very much required. As with the environment, we woke up after committing very many great disasters, let us not repeat a similar crime against the children.

—Contributed by Rajalakshmi

We need to face up to the challenges. Not hurry up as it occurs in the title. This situation cannot be allowed to continue. But what are the difficulties in countering this problem? It has been aptly stated that even the liberated generation has been naive in permitting the present practices to go unquestioned. Content of what children watch is very significant. Visual violence will never do good for the kids.

In contrast, there is significant effort to push internet technology into schools and claims to produce techno-smart children. While the industry is churning out educational applications and setting up techno schools, such experiments in the USA which started with great fanfare are reportedly closing down their practices, despite of enormous profits.

The techie buzz words are 'marketing mode' and are declared, social and emotional learning, mindset, grit, STEM, mindfulness, authentic learning and global consciousness'. These need to be dealt with, with scepticism. Some commonplace guide lines:

Sexual content at young age will never be good for kids (total entertainment on screen of any gadget).

No screens for children below two.

Limit two hours for a day for older children.

Children may learn something from visual media, but they learn 20 times better from parents.

Electronic time should not crowd out other parts of childhood (Strasburger, March 2016, *New York Times).*

Most parents do notice that the glowing screens have negative effect on their children. They have seen children responding aggressively, with temper tantrums when the devices are taken away, they have poor attention span and need continuous hyper stimulation. When not using the devices they become bored, uninterested and consequently not interesting company of either children or adults.

According to the 2013 policy statement by the American Academy of Paediatrics, 8 to 10 years olds spend 8 hours a day while teenager spend 11 hours a day in front of the digital screens. It is as serious as an addiction as drugs or alcohol. It needs detoxification and complete withdrawal of the toxic digital shift. This may require complete stoppage of all digital stuff for 4 to 6 weeks, till the hyper aroused nervous system resets itself. This includes television ban as well.

There should be a growing need for awareness and studies on children and adolescents in all the domains of normal development.

How does one prevent this addiction?

1. Stop them from getting hooked on to digital devices (do not give them the devices till they are 10 or even 12).

2. Substitute with the old-fashioned games of Legos instead of mind craft, board games instead of iPods and so on. Obviously, return to the kind of games children played in the good old days.

3. Do not use them as substitute for the parents actively engaging children through talk, games, songs, having dinner together (without the presence of the ubiquitous television). When parents-children have fun together, talking, playing, singing together it is called 'Quality Time'. Digital dose should be replaced with quality time, family and friends.
4. You have to explain to them why you are depriving them of the digital devices as these cause addiction. You need to explain how it affects the brain.

My Own Observations as a Child Psychologist

An infant seeks physical proximity of the mother, like it happens in the animal world. There is the learning from the famous studies of Harry Harlow of baby monkeys seek bodily warmth and closeness of the mother. Observations by John Bowlby on maternal deprivation and studies by Mary Ainsworth's on bonding and attachment behaviour offer insights into mother-child bonding. Bowlby's contribution is a unique one. The babies that do not have **maternal bonding and secure attachment** grow up to be individuals who are withdrawn, asocial with inability develop attachments.

When we use a gadget to replace this first stage of the infant and the mother bonding, things go awry. Either you prop a bottle in the baby's mouth or the mother feeds the baby more in tune with the cell phone posture rather than comfort of the baby. These are the first indications that the mother and child live in two separate worlds. With the slightly older child, the mother gives a mobile to the child rather than a traditional rattle! When the child starts to talk, his companion is a television or an iPad. One of the newspaper reports says, an occupational therapist has concluded that speech is delayed because children are hooked on to mobiles. These devices replace actual mothering.

Two-dimensional and Three-dimensional World

In my work with tribal children earlier, I observed something strange in the world of the first generation of literacy. When I showed a picture of man sitting on a chair to a child and asked what it was, the child could not answer. If I showed him the teacher sitting on a chair in the class room, he would say, 'Teacher is sitting on a chair'. I found out that for these children who had never seen an illustrated book before, it took a while to understand the two-dimension reality. They also had trouble in arranging picture in a sequential format. But once they become familiar with reading, this problem disappeared. In contrast, recently I showed a girl of two years of age, a picture of an animal, she held the picture and tried to expand the picture in the middle to make it bigger as she does, while seeing pictures on the mobile screen!

The above two experiences caused me a great concern. *By using these devices, are we converting the three-dimensional world into a two-dimensional world without realising that brain functioning is being altered even with this common place gadget?*

In the three-dimensional world we have inputs from the environment which reaches the brain through sensory modalities: visual, auditory, tactile, gustatory kinaesthetic and olfactory sensations, tuning the brain to assimilate and accommodate the real environment. If the child lets go of the three-dimensional and uses more of the two-dimensional input, he will have trouble separating **reality** from the **virtual reality**.

I believe we are creating a **virtual reality** which **actually replaces reality**. This has serious implications to child development in all the domains. Technology cannot substitute real life learning, especially in children and adolescents in the critical phase of their development.

I believe this will not only lead to digital addiction but also to mental health problems, difficulty in acquiring learning skills, empathetic interpersonal skills and communication. When a digital success or failure by the way of reward or punishment weighs on you more than real reward or punishment, you become a 'misfit' in the real world.

Solution? Simple. Let children play as they have done since time immemorial. Technology can be appreciated only when you have a mature brain!

The first question is how does the child understand and what does he see?

How does a 3-year-old see and understand a fight between two people?

How does a 6-year-old see and understand killing and destroying, as seen in cartoons?

How does a 9-year-old see and understand and be influenced by an aggressive video game?

Once we ask ourselves these questions, then we will understand how the indiscriminate viewing of television programmes, mobile clippings, websites, YouTube and pornography affect children.

Saturation of any input leads to jadedness and be it aggressive or sexual content, there is a growing demand for excessive and indiscriminate inputs. The more you see, the less it affects you. Example: Inflicting pain on someone: first you may sympathise, later you may start enjoying it. For example, how popular is shooting and killing in most of the games?

Aggression in the media, be it in the various serials, competitions too are viewed differently by young children. Is there an adult available to objectively explain it to the children? No! So, the lesson is that if you use aggression to get what you want, it is justified.

The parents' role as the ones responsible for the development of conscience (or morality) is gradually fading. The child is at the mercy of various visual media or equally ill-equipped peer group.

Technology and the Child

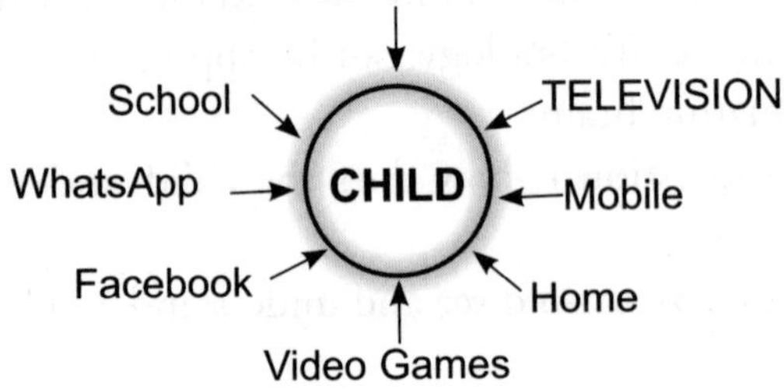

Shrinking Space for Normal and Real Human Interactions

In the near future, the boundary between what is 'real' and what is 'virtual' will become invisible. It is important that we keep the real world intact and keep the unreal world at bay.

Real caring and sharing happens at home and at school. But technology offers only dramatic pretend-sharing. Actual interaction at emotional-, social-interaction levels lead to maturity of the mind, while we do not actually know the actual impact of technology on the child's brain and mind.

A simple example, a 2-year-old is holding on to her mother's leg crying out, 'Mummy, mummy, I want to tell you something'. But the mother pushes her and says,'I am on the phone!'. How can there be bonding between the two? What the child is trying to tell her is of no consequence. It could be a most ubiquitous needless call of a person from telemarketing, gaining the mother's attention.

Why should a phone call take priority over a real interaction?

This holds true for children as well as adults. The child is trying to touch the mother, indicating she wants her physical contact. But the mother does not recognise it. In an ideal situation, the child calls out and the mother picks her up and they proceed to have a conversation where the mother discovers her child and the child feels comforted in her company. This bonding is what child and mother is about!

I have seen young mothers giving their children their mobiles instead of 'rattles' to keep them amused. Of course, being smart, they press all the right keys and learn the functional skills of using this particular object. But if she gives the child a rattle, a leaf, an empty cup, a ball, a piece of cloth, he would learn about how to wave a rattle and make sounds, feel the texture, smell and taste of the leaf. Mother could actually say 'green' so he learns the name of a colour, an empty cup can be filled with water or sand, filled, emptied and transferred, a ball can be thrown and fetched, a piece of cloth can be used to wipe the face or make a flag. Children love feeling different textures on their bodies.

By giving a cell phone to a child, the mother fails to enable the child to connect to the world around him! To sum up, use of technology with children below two years age is dangerous, and with older children it should be judiciously used. *But technology is no substitute for warm and affectionate human interaction in childhood.*

The turn of the century has seen many digital advocates positively affirm the role of video games in brain development and dexterity. Video games are supposed to improve attention and concentration and problem-solving skills. Video games also enhance computer literacy and an understanding of graphics, design and animation.

For all these positive effects, there are more number of downsides to allowing children screen time with video games.

The American Association of Pediatrics (AAP) does not recommend screen time in any form (television, mobile, video games) for children below two. The AAP strongly advises parents/guardians to limit media usage for children until they are able to self-limit their own usage.

Yet, in India we find the ubiquitous mobile play the role of a 'digital nanny' in many families. A wailing child (whether 3 months or 3 years) is often given a mobile to distract him and calm him down. What an irony! Young children who cannot understand the basics of a game are often just attracted by the snazzy colours and lights on the mobile. They quickly learn to play with it as they grow and soon play music and get hooked on to mobile games. Instead of going outside and engaging in physical play, children are glued to their mobiles and video games.

A mindless activity, which hardly encourages critical thinking! This form of media use can be addictive as we ourselves notice as adults our obsession with our mobiles. How many times do we check our mobile screens for messages or missed calls during the day and night!

Digital Nannies: Video Games and Children's Entertainment

Video game playing clearly interferes with children's reading habits and outdoor play. Visit any apartment in Bangalore and you will be more likely to catch groups of children texting or playing mobile games instead of outdoor games! Mindless consumption of entertainment seems to fit in with people as they prefer to thrust a mobile into the hands of their children to entertain them quietly instead of actively engaging with them.

Constructive activities like board games, learning to play musical instruments, reading books and newspapers and all other outdoor activities like gardening or just playing have taken a backseat. Even family conversations have become rarer as each is glued to his/her personal screen space. A grim sign of our times!

An Anecdotal Account

In my own experience as a child, a brief stint with video games did me little good. When I was 6 years old, I was given a Super Nintendo video game console which came pre-loaded with several games and the popular 'Duck Hunt'. This was a light gun zapper to shoot ducks that came on the screen. Of course, it involved quick reflexes and the ability to shoot down the creatures as they flew across the screen. I was thrilled with the hunting game and soon became addicted, often gobbling my dinner to go and shoot ducks.

I also became selfish and refused to share my game with other kids and playmates. Soon my mother realised the folly of giving me this form of entertainment and took it away. I was very angry and threw tantrums, but my mother was firm and refused to let me play. Slowly I got over this addiction and adjusted into other activities, spending more time reading and outdoors. When I look back, I remember my days with the video game sitting alone and playing, with no social interaction with other kids. I gained little and, in the bargain, landed with eye strain and general restlessness.

My attention levels in all other activities took a beating as I always had the duck hunt at the back of my mind, thinking up strategies to shoot more ducks. I was restless and according to my mother became very aggressive as somehow the use of the gun affected my self-image. I also became selfish and refused to share my game with other kids and playmates.

—Contributed by Namitha Kumar

There have been extensive studies on this kind of excessive media use which leads to attention deficit issues, hyperactivity, restlessness, sleep disorders and obesity. Video game playing clearly interferes with children's reading habits and outdoor play. Visit any apartment in Bangalore and you will be more likely to catch groups of children texting or playing mobile games instead of outdoor games! Mindless consumption of entertainment seems to fit in with people as they prefer to thrust a mobile onto their children to entertain them quietly instead of actively engaging with them. Constructive activities like board games, learning to play musical instruments, reading books and newspapers and all other outdoor activities like gardening or just playing have taken a backseat. Even family conversations have become rarer as each is glued to his/her personal screen space. A grim sign of our times!

The ASER 2017 survey in India has shown, more than seven of 10 in the age group of 14-18 used a cell phone but a quarter of them cannot read basic text fluently in their own language. It is the property of association that works. The survey, which also looked at the understanding of the youth's access to media, financial institutions and digital world, found 73 per cent of the youth had used a mobile phone. Here, too, the gender differences are glaring. As against 12 per cent boys who had never used a mobile phone, the number of girls for the same was higher – 22 per cent.

Some years ago, a popular DVD called *Baby Einstein* was very vigorously marketed and sold in millions to the aspirational new parents in the USA. Subsequently, a psychological impact study showed that it did not benefit the children who viewed them and, in some cases, affected them adversely! The company withdrew the product from the market and reimbursed the amount.

The caution about technology, toys and objects is that, these are produced by adults who imagine from their perspective what a child's world would be like and create the toys. If they had real insight and compassion, they would not make this grotesque aggressive game where the only thing to be enhanced is reaction time and give rise to lot of negative feelings and the notion one must always WIN otherwise one is a LOSER! For example, the child believes that he must win, and he must be appreciated all the time. If he does not win, he is no good and others will make fun of him. When only winning becomes important, the feelings of others (all the losers) are not important. There is no empathy for other people's feelings when a child is being hurt, other children want to watch the fun as if it is a game, with no empathy for the victim. One does not try to rescue or help him. In fact, the child may join the crowd to watch the fun.

Nicholas Kardaras in 2016 called this addiction in young children as 'digital heroin'. He says that iPods, smart phones and Xboxes are a form of digital drug. He cites several case studies of children and calls them 'psychotic junkies'.

Most tech-conscious parents are tech designers and engineers. Likewise, Silicon Valley parents are hi-tech parents. They are aware of the dangers they are letting loose on the children of the world but protect their own children!

Technologies blur the boundary between what is **real** and is **not real**. They also arouse emotions that are inappropriate and immature responses, when one has to respond to real life situations. The growing brain adopts itself to an unreal world and consequently fails to develop surviving skills in the real world.

Now we are faced with the question of how to prevent the aftermath of the genie being let out of the bottle. There have been successful campaigns against smoking, which has resulted in reduced incidence of smoking amongst youth in the West. There have been successful campaigns against drunken driving.

But both the above dangers are associated with physical proofs of damage caused. But especially with children and adolescent, most research is anecdote. But it is very hard to prove negative psychological impact with empirical research. By the time we get those results it might be too late to contain the damage that has already occurred to an entire generation. On the extreme end we have Robot(AI) nannies, Alexa for example,who can manipulate the minds of their young wards and replace their mothers and turn them into strangers or even adults into idiots when compared to Alexa!

Awareness of Children

1. There are awareness programmes such as 'About Tech', 'Common Sense' and 'Humane Technology' designed to expose the ways that platforms like YouTube, Facebook, Snapchat are harmful to children and these programmes protect young minds from digital manipulation.
2. Parental supervision and control. This requires parent sensitisation and parental sensitivity and parental skills and effective communication with children. There may be applications for parental control, but these are afterthoughts of the techno-industry, after reports of negative fallout of their gimmicks and digital control through addictive properties of the games/activities surface.
3. Taking the child into confidence and have a relationship where the parent may support the child to overcome the addiction and take him to the places where there are centres for the treatment of internet addictions.
4. Peer discussions with an informed adult, who is not addicted himself, to help them come out before it is too late.

5. Schools too need to recognise the need for containing the digital and to be sensitised.
6. Is it too much to expect that techno-industry not harm people, especially children? The robot nannies are already proposing to replace the real mothers! After all the GPS has already shrunk our ability to navigate in the real world. What a contrast to the famous study of the brains of the old time British taxi drivers with their phenomenal memory for all the roads and addresses in and around London!

PART IV
CHILD HIMSELF

14

Child Development and Care

IN THIS chapter an attempt is made to bridge the gap between Western developmental psychology and child care practices in ancient India.

Child Development

Child's development occurs simultaneously on seven domains. These are in **physical, intellectual, language, emotional, social, moral** and **sexual realms.**

Overall development in the above domains occur differently along the different developmental phases at different ages. For example, the physical development at three months is different from what he can do at six months, nine months or one year, from birth to the age of 12 years. There are dramatic changes that occur, in the brain as well as physical development of the child. These in turn affect all the developmental domains. These can be enhanced or warped, depending on what happens in the physical and socio-cultural contexts.

Some people believe that the nature of a child is entirely determined by **Heredity.** Others believe that all these are due to **Environment.**

Psychological and sociological theories and research provides us with answers. Yet these insights are misused by politicians or society for its own benefit. An environmentalist famously said,'Give me a child, I can make him an idiot or genius'. On the other hand, all societies believe race, class and caste differences as inborn and unchangeable. Both these are right and wrong. Child development occurs equally because of heredity and environment. It is not EITHER or OR.

Maturation and **Learning** are two other ingredients of promoting development. Both promote development and not either or.

The body and the brain maturation is key to development, yet learning enhances development equally. There are critical stages in development. The infant or the child should reach optimal level of maturation before he can attain some of the skills. Be it sitting, walking or speaking in the normal course of time. A 6-month old can be propped on a baby walker and made to walk. But when he is 9 to 12 month sold, he will walk by himself. Why the hurry?

A preschool child loves to play for hours together. But we want them to read, write and do sums and finally achieve it by constant pressure by the adults. But why the hurry? Upon maturation these skills can be learnt quickly and effectively. The samskara of Upanayana recommends that the introduction of scholastic skills may start around 7 years. Babies swaddled for two years in some cultures, and others who are left free, all start walking around the same time. Maturation is a process we should keep in mind when we pressurise children to learn what we want them to learn.

The other component is **motivation**. A child can learn less or more, prompted by motivation. This could be self motivated like the 'Scientist in the crib', prompted by imitation or encouragement by others.

In taking care of our children we can examine the above from three perspectives.

1. 1,000–2,000 years ago, in ancient India what were the concepts and practices? There is an Ayurveda treatise named *Kashyapa Samhita* that provides several insights into child development and child care.
2. What are the contemporary views on child development based on Western theories and research?
3. In the last three decades, many new insights have emerged based on actual research on children as they grow up and pass through various phases of development. I am trying to introduce you to this miracle called the child.

I have named these phases along the thinking of researchers in the last three decades.

1. Abhimanyu (Baby/Foetus in the Womb)
2. Scientist in the Crib/Cradle: From Birth to Three Years
3. Wandering Scholar: From Three to Six Years
4. Victorious: From Six Years to Eleven Years

In all the above stages, there are multifaceted developments across the seven domains. The child needs at each phase of development adequate care. Let us examine the needs of the child in each of the above stages

1. Abhimanyu

Western thinkers have described the newborns' mind as 'clean state' – consists of 'blooming buzzing confusion'. The implication is that we teach the child everything, like writing on a clean state. You all are familiar with the story of Abhimanyu. The unborn Abhimanyu was supposed to have learnt how to enter the Chakravyuha as told to Subadhra by Krishna. In *Kashyapa Samhita*, the foetus is described to be growing rapidly not only physically but also intellectually and socially and responding and reacting to what is happening to the mother or even in the environment.

Consequently, in Ayurveda, the foetus and the pregnant woman are considered as a single unit. Soon after birth the same bonding continues. At the third month there is awareness of pain and happiness, in the fourth month there is consciousness, in the fifth month the mind emerges and in the

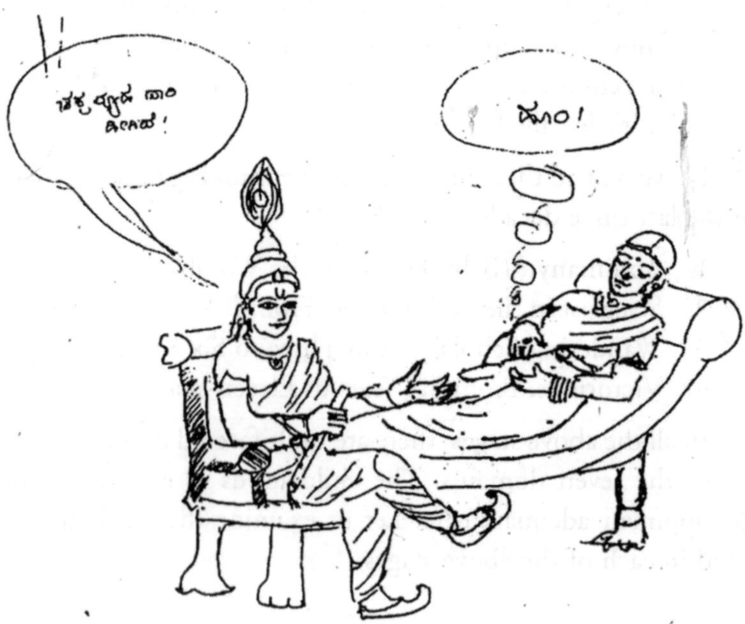

sixth month intelligence becomes manifest. The eighth month is a tumultuous time for the foetus and the newborn is not a clean state but a fully responsive being.

What is astounding is that the experiments and observations of newborns, infants and young children reveal that he is conscious, alert, attended to the environment soon after birth. His learning and responding appropriately to the mother and the environment, shows that he is endowed with potential to learn rapidly and adjust to the environment. Because of the sensitive nature of the foetus, woman is extended a special status along with rituals, to keep her healthy and happy so that the infant too is healthy when he is born. From the seventh month, after the '*Simmantonanyana*' samskara, the pregnant woman goes to the maternal home to be taken care of. How long she stays there in this protected stress-free environment, depends on the cultural practices of different communities.

In the present day, maternal homes are, along the Western medical practice, not considered essential or important. In EEC recordings, the foetus, as a part of maternal physical and psychological wellbeing, has shown being affected in the foetal and maternal brain, if the mother is compromised in any way. The newborn baby of an alcoholic mother is born manifesting 'foetal alcohol syndrome'.

2. Scientist in the Crib

After birth, studies have revealed that the newborn tracks light and closely observes the environment. Soon enough, he responds to mother's voice and recognises her face (but not a mask). In fact, responds with a smile when she smiles! With different kinds of cries, his mother can make out whether he is hungry, wet or sleepy. This is the beginning of emotional relationship and communication which appears within a week of birth.

The infant also has inherited tendency for emotionality. It is called 'temperament' and will be described in the next chapter. At each stage from infancy the child has different physical, intellectual and psychological needs. For example, young infant needs to be held and cuddled. Physical warmth and closeness is needed. This allows the infant to bond with the mother physically and psychologically.

Of course, it is important to note that mother's personality and infant's temperament need to match. Otherwise, there will be interactional difficulties. An irritable mother will react adversely to an irritable child. If the infant is happy and placid, the mother would not have any trouble taking care of it. In the West, three simple categories of temperament described are: Easy Child, Difficult Child and Slow to Warm Child (Thomas and Chess). On the other hand, in ancient Indian practice, the temperament/personality traits are described as Triguna consisting of Satvik, Rajasik and Tamasik. But the inherent thinking is that though these are present at birth these can be modified by training or experience. This is in agreement with the notion that heredity and environment are equally important in child development.

Let us, for example, observe the six-month-old scientist. He examines the environment and learns from it even before he starts learning to speak. An infant exposed to speech or music before six months of age, has deeper grasp of the same, if he continues with it thereafter. A music teacher who was giving lessons to her students with her young son on the lap, noticed that he would go to sleep when a student sang well but get restless and irritable if someone sang off tune.

Even language skills come easily to them at this stage. You may have seen 2–3 years old talking in three different languages with different relatives or children.

This is because the infant is born 'prewired for language' acquisition (Chomsky). The child constantly tries to understand the world by observing, touching and experimenting with each and everything in the environment. This is when mother starts shouting 'Don't – Don't' for everything. Playing in mud or water, running, jumping and fall are all natural part of growing up. They want to know 'Why?' of everything and parents do not answer because they think, he is only a child and children do not need to know everything. In fact, an ideal parent should answer every question. If he does not know, he will have to find out the right answer for the child.

Most often, the child wants to feed himself, bathe himself and dress himself when very young. But for variety of reasons, the parents like to do it for them. At this critical stage, if the child is not allowed to learn the self-help skills, he will later on manipulate his parents and get them to do all his work But doing everything for the child is the sure way to warp his overall development self-help skills.

Most mothers indulge in these activities, believing that they are being good mothers. Many mothers in India are responsible for feeding and eating problems and overdependency in their children. A child of three wants to be an independent human being. To promote his overall development, she needs to let him go.

3. Wandering Scholar (3–6 Years)

At this stage, the child wants to separate from the mother and become independent. He wants to spend time playing with other children or observe nature and explore. He thinks a great deal and wants to understand the world. He feels empathy when someone is sad or upset and tries to soothe them. If you pay attention to a child's questions, you will understand how deeply he thinks. Jivaka had so many profound observations to make.

Often, mothers being protective do not allow their children to play with others, citing reasons, getting hurt, learning bad things from bad children and so on. Children must play and learn how to live amicably with others.

4. Victorious Adventurer (6–12 Years)

Once the child joins school his entire life changes. He enters a world with strangers—other children, teachers and other school staff. They do not pamper the child like they do at home. Your family is not with you to support. Initially many children are fearful, cry and do not want to go to school. But mostly, they settle down and adjust to the school environment. Before the school, for a variety of reasons, parents send their children to preschools these days. In India sadly, most preschools are sad places to be in. Ideally the children are expected to spend their entire time in play. Instead they are made to read, write and do number work. This is totally against the principles of normal child development.

Play is the only activity that promotes overall development.

All learning/teaching in India in preschools and regular schools follow only **teacher-centred method.** It entirely depends on teachers teaching to learn by rote and copying. There is no scope for play or individual enjoyable activities.

As seen in this chapter, a child is born full of creative potential. He is a scientist, philosopher and adventurous. He is not given the freedom to be what he is. He is forced to learn mechanically, by rote, repeatedly boring subjects, while the world is full of challenges and enjoyable objects. **Let us move from teacher/adult-centered learning to child-centered learning.**

15

Nature of the Child

IN THE previous chapters, the focus has been entirely on the impact of the environment on the growth and development of the child. You would obviously be wondering what the role of the child is in all these situations. It is true that the child is the key player and who he is and what he is matter a great deal.

The child is born with certain physical, psychological and behavioural characteristics. These could be due to combined influence of biological events or psychological dispositions. **The question is not whether it is hereditary or due to the environment. It is actually a combination of both.** In chapters 1 to 13 the focus was on environment. This shows how important the environment is for the development of a child.

But the child brings with him the potential for learning, interacting and communicating effectively with the environment.

So, we need to know what the infant brings with him when he is born. These have been discussed in earlier chapters.

The child comes with:

1. Biological Vulnerabilities
2. Intellectual Potential
3. Emotional Disposition or Temperament
4. Psychological Disorders

The child is born with the above overlapping characteristics to varying degrees. Any deficits in any one of the above potentials puts the child at risk. This is even more so if the environment is non-congenial or even harmful.

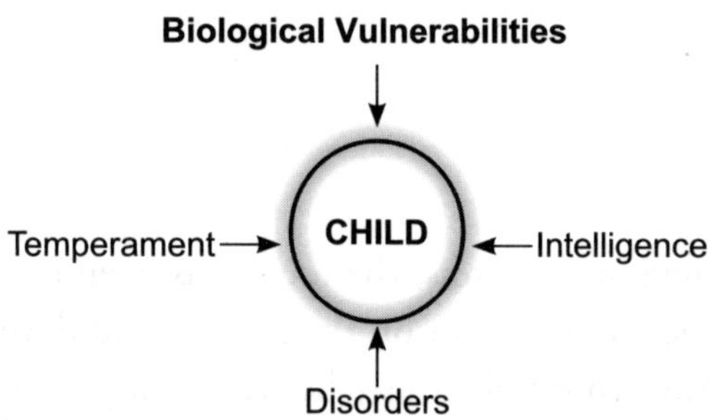

Biological Vulnerabilities

The deficits may occur at the foetal stage, before or after birth. At the foetal stage, maternal malnutrition, ill health or even emotional distress may cause problems to the foetus. Addiction to drugs or alcohol in the mother may predispose the newborn to drug or alcohol dependencies. There could be medical complications during pregnancy, before or after child birth, to the mother. Consequently, the infant may be exposed to different types of trauma. An example of how a medical procedure may be misused is abundantly clear in Indian society. A scan for testing the health of the foetus is being misused to terminate female foetus, though illegal. This has led to skewed population ratios in many of the Indian States.

The other is the 'caesarean section' being used for non-medical reasons. For example, firm believers in horoscopes demand auspicious time for birth to be arranged sometimes, though the mother is capable of healthy and normal child birth. At other times a mother capable of normal birth may opt for caesarean section for fear of pain. It could be for the obstetrician's convenience more than for the health of the mother or the child. But it is a fact that caesarean section is not good for the newborn because of the sudden arrival into the outside world, instead of gradual easing and moving into it. These infants carry some risks to development.

Caesarean sections should be done only when there are medical indications to suggest dangers to the mother or the foetus. Seeking medical procedure for trivial reasons is wrong.

In addition to issues of health,the newborn infant may have minor or serious brain trauma, high fever, epileptic fits, head injury or may even be born with underdeveloped brain. This infant is at risk for other disorders too.

Intelligence

Children are born with different intellectual potential. Very few are of very low intelligence (as measured by tests and converted into IQ quotients). But 2/3 of all children fall in the average range and some in the superior range.

What is important to remember is that though the majority of children fall in the average range, yet some of them may not show academic skills appropriate to their intellectual potential. The reasons for the potential not being converted into actual performance are many.

To cite a few:

- Deprived home or institutional environment

- Very poor schooling
- Psychological disorders (Attention Deficit, Hyperactivity Disorder, Learning Disorder, Emotion Disorder, Conduct Disorder etc)
- Extreme pressure to perform or excel in studies/sports etc

Thus, to promote intelligence, one needs to remove the obstacles that come in the way of realising the child's full intellectual potential.

However, intelligence is not one unique endowment. There are specific and multiple intelligences of different kinds. Creativity and imagination manifests in different ways. One could be a scientist, an artist, a musician, a writer and so on.

Temperament

Temperament is the emotional disposition the infant is born with. In ancient Indian tradition, this is called *Triguna* and it consists of Satvik, Rajasik and Tamasik nature. Even young children have these emotional predispositions. Some of the descriptions are given below.

Psychosocial	Satvik	Rajasik	Tamasik
Easy to manage	Mostly	Not at all	Somewhat
Independent (can manage himself/herself)	Mostly	Somewhat	Not at all
Dependable	Mostly	Somewhat	Not at all
Sensitive (to others needs, Emotions)	Mostly	Somewhat	Not at all
Sensitive (only about oneself)	Somewhat	Mostly	Not at all
Trusting	Mostly	Somewhat	Not at all
Trustworthy	Mostly	Somewhat	Not at all
Moral (discriminates between good and bad. Knows it is bad to hit others, steal, etc)	Mostly	Somewhat	Not at all
Bio-social			
Sleep	Moderate	Too little	Too much
Appetite	Moderate	Too little	Too much
Activity	Moderate	Too little	Too much
Emotionality	Cheerful Angry/Tense	Dull (Non-reactive)	
Persistence	Good	Variable	Too little
Sociability with family members	Adequate	Mostly	Not at all
Sociability with others outside	Adequate	Mostly	Not at all
Aggression (verbal)	Not at all	Mostly	Somewhat
Aggression (physical)	Not at all	Mostly	Somewhat

The child comes into the world with a mixture of the above characteristics. If most of the characteristics are under Satvik, the child may be considered a Satvik child. Similarly, predominance of Rajas or Tamas too can indicate if the child is Rajasik or Tamasik.

The above classification supports the notion once again, that the child is born with a temperament which is unique to him. It is not taught by us. But interaction with the environment can modify it. If a restless child is cared for by an irritable mother, his behaviour worsens. If an irritable infant is soothed by a calm mother, the child becomes calmer as well. Most of us fail to recognise that each child has different nature and personality.

Brain Disorders that Affect Psychological Development

Brain Trauma Due To

- Epilepsy (fits)
- Meningitis (very high fever)
- Head injury
- Any other disorder affecting the brain

Developmental Delays or Disorders (not crawling, sitting, walking or speaking at appropriate time)

- Delay in motor development
- Delay or disorders of language development (stammering, inability to talk clearly, etc)
- Delay in gaining bladder/bowel control
- Poor physical coordination or clumsiness
- Delays involving all the above: mental retardation or some of the above: Autism where overall development remains compromised
- Disorders related to routine habits such as sleep or feeding

Attention Deficit and Hyperactivity Disorder (ADHD)

- Poor attention
- Distractibility or getting distracted easily
- Over activity and always moving around
- Impulsivity – acts without thinking, like not paying attention to traffic or other dangers or pushing or hitting other children without any provocation

These children are observed to be quick and over-active as soon as they start walking. However, these symptoms may be present in some situations (for example only at home, only at schools or while visiting someone). This is called situational hyperactivity. It is related to how the child is managed by those around. It happens when someone is very strict or very lax. These children misbehave when they know that they can get away with it. However, some children are persistently overactive, inattentive and impulsive regardless of where they are. This is a disorder and the child needs to be taken to a child counsellor or child psychologist or a child psychiatrist. Such children need training for reducing over activity and improving attention. In extreme cases, they may need medication to control the symptoms if they are very severe.

Out of Control Child

Satvik is a nine-year-old boy with the complaints of poor performance, disturbing the class, always moving around and being very stubborn since he was 4 years old.

On observation: he was very overactive and had learning difficulties. The family history revealed that he was pampered as a child and there was inconsistent disciplining. Early developmental details showed that the mother was very depressed and lonely and had felt inferior when she was pregnant. The family lived in a foreign country during her pregnancy, child birth and early developmental stages of the child. The mother herself did not have any chance for socialisation. The mother was on medication for some time for depression. She always felt inferior as she was not able to speak English. She had a very dominating mother-in-law who was critical of her which led to further reduction in confidence. Due to above reasons, the mother was not able to feed the child well and she had felt guilty about it. Solving the problem needed work with the mother by building up her confidence levels and changing the child's behaviour.

In addition to the mother's problem, the father too suffered from a muscular problem which made him very weak sometimes and he was not able to support mother in the child's upbringing.

The above factors reveal that the child had lack of stimulation when he needed it the most. He also learnt to manipulate and take advantage of the weakness of the parents and indulge in disruptive behaviour with others.

Satvik's strength is that he is very creative. He was able to tell his views through his drawings. He used to draw new things, and, in every drawing, he showed some new inventions in the technology. He was very imaginative which reflected in his drawings. He was not colouring his drawings as he felt that it was not needed and that he was not able to give the extra attention needed for colouring. It was seen that his impulsivity and attention deficiency compelled him not to complete his works.

The child was given simple tasks like sorting grains, beading, colouring which required very little of his time. His mother was convinced to send him to play outdoor games under supervision and he was also encouraged to play indoor games with his mother, to help her to come out of her diffidence. He got rewarded for the expected behaviour and this was done with the consensus of the family and the child.

—Contributed by Arathi Rao

Conduct Disorders

These children have the following symptoms:

- Stubbornness
- Disobedience
- Often interrupting others playing, talking, being disruptive while playing, or breaking/throwing things frequently
- Quarrelsomeness and fighting
- Aggression as seen by hitting, biting and pinching others (with/without provocation)
- Getting angry, crying a lot, rolling on the ground and continuing to be so for a long time, when his/her demands are not met (temper tantrums)
- Going to school and coming back on time, but actually not attending the school
- Indulging in lying and cheating

If a child **occasionally** does any of the above activities, it is not considered a disorder. But if many of the symptoms are present over a period of time, it is time to take the child for consultation as these children are very hard to manage at home. At times, parents become helpless and give in to the child's demands and thus lead to worsening of behaviour. Or parents react with extreme anger and severely punish the child. Neither are proper ways of dealing with the situation.'Gentle setting of limits' is needed.

Anomalous Family with a Difficult Child

Hari was in ninth standard and was brought with the complaint that he lies and has started stealing at home and school. He was a good-looking, shy natured boy. He was given some activities like drawing etc. while the counsellors talked to the parents to learn the details about his birth and development. Hari currently has a step father. This was the second marriage of both his mother and step-father.

Since her husband was a drunkard and bad person, Hari's mother left her husband and was living in her mother's place until Hari was 10. As there was no one in their life for almost five years, mother and son had a strong bonding without the need of anyone else. Because of financial difficulty and a desire to give better education to Hari, mother decided to get remarried and she got a divorce from her husband.

The second man's wife had run away with someone within a week of their marriage, the man was living alone. He was from a joint family and was very orthodox. Everyone related to him only for his money. He also knew this but carried on with them as he didn't have anybody else. According to him, he had a wish to run an orphanage. Then he had a thought that if he married a lady already having a child, he could provide a better life for that child. This was the intention behind them both getting remarried.

It was one year after their remarriage. Hari was in a boarding school. The step-father neither talked to Hari nor his mother. Though they were not talking to each other, the wife understood the husband's dominating nature. Since he had to take responsibility at an early age, he became dominating. Because of his work in the transport business, he had become rude. He was behaving in a harsh way with the family, just like the way he behaved with his employees. Hari's mother had a lot of dreams about this marriage, naturally, as her previous marriage was a disaster. She had an expectation of living like a loving couple shown in cinemas.

He was not able to satisfy this because of the large age gap and also because of his over-disciplinary nature. She could not share this with him and started suffering inwardly, which resulted in anger, intolerance and histrionic behaviour in her. In a dilemma between the feelings of gratitude for the life he gave her and feelings of frustration at not being able to lead her dream life, she spent one year.

Initially it was difficult for the step-father also to adjust to this new life. He was very particular about cleanliness. Hari was brought back from boarding school and it was very difficult for him to adjust to this cleanliness. Parents began to fight. The step-father started teasing the boy for throwing things here and there.

Since mother was unable to either teach the boy or convince the husband, she started to beat the boy. Hari had to face punishments and disciplining episodes. He could not tolerate his mother being controlled by another person. Being brought up in poverty, suddenly when he saw money, Hari took some money to spend it with friends. Step-father called him a thief which provoked the boy. Both mother and Hari are hurt because of being repeatedly called a thief. The step-father's over-disciplining even regarding how to sit, what to eat and wear, has created problems for Hari. Mother is feeling helpless. All these have resulted in stealing and telling lies.

—Contributed by Harish Aatreya

Emotional Disorder

These are disorders in children wherein the child suffers quietly and does not complain about anything. Conduct disordered children cause **distress** and **anger** in **others.** The emotionally disordered children do not bother others but suffer in silence. Some of the symptoms are:

- Refusing to go to school and staying back home for a duration of weeks or months
- Day dreaming
- Being very quiet and reserved (withdrawn)
- Talking very little even with family members
- Worrying
- Anxiousness and nervousness

- Shyness and timidity
- Is fearful of animals/situations
- Clinging
- Crying easily

Adults often fail to notice the distress of the child and praise the child as a quiet and good child. Once again, if the symptoms are severe the child has difficulty in relating to people at home or outside. If he is very quiet and withdrawn to the extent that even the school performance suffers and the withdrawn nature of the child is commented upon by others, it is a sign of stress.

Problems in School

Bhoomika is an eight-year-old girl studying in 3rd standard English medium school. She is the first child with a younger brother of three. Her father is an engineer and mother has done her masters. Recently mother has quit her job to take care of the two kids. Bhoomika is very much attached to her paternal grandmother.

Bhoomika is a shy and sensitive child. She was brought with the complaints of low performance in school since 1st standard. She was slow in writing and in doing her daily work. She had started getting irritated and aggressive since the past 6 months.

In the clinic, initially, the child was quiet and clinging to her mother. She liked to draw and colour. She looked very happy while drawing. She was very imaginative. Except for her slow writing speed, she had no difficulties in academics.

The child was always compared and punished by her teacher in her nursery class (when she was 4 years). This could have lowered her confidence. The mother was upset with the teacher and changed the school.

The child got adjusted to new school but even today she felt scared to talk to teachers. Inconsistent disciplining by the parents also made the child feel low emotionally.

As the father was exceptionally strict about discipline and the child was needy for the mother's affection which she did not receive, it reflected on her studies. She became more aggressive and expressed it by hitting her younger brother.

The parents were counselled. They took it positively and visible improvements were seen in the child's behaviour.

Also, tasks on time management were assigned as she was slow in day-to-day activities. A caring and affectionate home tutor helped in building the confidence of the child and this in turn brought a major change in her academic performance. Successive counselling sessions took place to analyse the child's improvement through her drawings, a medium she was comfortable expressing through.

—Contributed by Veena Suresh

Conduct disorder and emotional disorder appear to be at the two extreme ends. But most children may have some features from both disorders. These are very common forms of disorders of childhood.

There is yet one more disorder where the child repeatedly indulges in an action to avoid anxiety. This is called Obsessive Compulsive Disorder and may occur rarely in childhood. Example: Going on doing a particular thing over and over again, such as washing hands, or repeatedly saying certain numbers, or expressing that certain thoughts come to his mind repeatedly to the extent that it interferes with his/her daily activities.

Learning Disorders

Learning disorders are commonly encountered in the school settings. These may be because of the poor school systems as described in the school section of the book or may be due to inherent learning difficulties in the child. This disorder is called `Specific Learning Disability' (SLD). It has to be seen in the following context. The child has:

- Normal intelligence
- Has no visual or hearing deficiencies. Has gone to a good school
- Is generally 2-3 years behind his class level

The symptoms commonly seen are:

- Poor school performance
- Difficulty in reading
- Difficulty in writing
- Difficulty in arithmetic
- Forgetfulness or poor memory
- Difficulties in comprehension of written material though spoken words are understood very well

The onset of SLD is always gradual and starts with early difficulties with alphabets and number. If drop in scholastic performance occurs suddenly, after several years of normal school performance, the reasons may be other kinds of psychological disturbance.

The child with SLD requires systematic remediation dealing with specific deficits detected during assessment. However, a child with SLD is likely to have other disorders as well. Be it ADHD, CD or ED.

Learning Disorder

Prajwal is a 15-year-old studying in class 10 in an English medium school. Prajwal is the only child. His father is a business man. Mother a home maker. He stays with his maternal aunt for completing his high school. He was brought with the complaints of low performance in academics. The boy was not allowed to take up board examinations as low grades may reflect badly on the institution. This refusal had affected the boy as he felt shunned by the institution he grew up studying in. The hostility took a toll on his confidence and he refused to take up board examination and remained as a high school dropout. His parents took him for counselling.

Prajwal was not very talkative. He looked sad and confused. He was a very good athlete and participated in inter school competitions and got various laurels for his institution in the field. There was a glow in his eyes when he started speaking about his favourite sports, that is cricket. He mentioned that Sachin Tendulkar was his inspiration. His only ambition was to excel in sports.

He also expressed his difficulty in the English subject and mathematics. The parents were worried more about the boy's future, though they were not particular about his grades in board examination. Also, his refusal to take up examination made them even more anxious. When asked about what could be the other option that the school suggests, they said he should appear as a private candidate.

The boy said he felt insulted and will be ridiculed by other classmates if they come to know about it. Through counselling sessions, he was made to understand that after $10^{th,}$ many of his classmates would join different courses as everyone had their own priorities in life. Hence, at present his aim was to take up the 10th exams. As he was a sports person, he accepted that finishing the game was more important.

Even his tuition teacher was involved and requested to encourage the boy till his examinations. Probably these supporting words made the boy feel confident and finally he accepted that he would sit for the examination privately.

He said, as his interest was in games and definitely not in academics, he would face the exam without any fear. He was in constant touch with the counsellor till the end of his examinations.

—Contributed by Veena Suresh

Physical Symptoms due to Psychological Distress/Stresses

The body and the mind interact and constantly influence each other. Psychological distress often manifests as bodily symptoms both in children as well as adults without any physical basis. These are as follows:

- Complaining of dizziness or giddiness
- Complaining of aches and pains
- Complaining of always feeling tired
- Complaining of stomach ache
- Fainting spells
- Attacks of jerky movements and unconsciousness (fits or convulsions to be differentiated from epilepsy by a clinician)
- Complaining of pulling sensation of the limbs

At times, instead of focussing on the symptoms, if one attends to the emotional distress, the physical symptoms may come down or disappear altogether. Often these children are repeatedly taken to the doctors. Despite several investigations no cause is found for these symptoms. That is why these are considered as due to psychological distress.

In addition, psychical disorders like asthama may worsen due to stress—body and mind being in constant interaction. The body speaks in its own way about the pain is felt in the mind.

Mental Disorders and Addictions

As children reach adolescence they may have mental disorders like adults or indulge in addiction of tobacco, drugs, alcohol and even the internet.

To conclude, the child comes into the world with some inborn deficits and advantages, in terms of biological, psychosocial and emotional predispositions. In a congenial environment the child will thrive.

In an adversarial environment, suffering is caused not only to the child but also to those around. But each child is an individual who needs to be cared for in a compassionate yet firm manner so that he fulfils his potential.

When you have a tied up bunch of flowering plants in your hand, it is not possible to identify which is the root of a particular flower by looking at the root or the flower, unless we untangle the bundle and separate the plants. *Similarly, only by going into the cause of what caused a symptom we can help the child.*

Only by unravelling the string you may find which plant comes of which root.

PART V
WHERE DO WE GO FROM HERE?

16

Silver Linings and Future Possibilities

HELPING CHILDREN in their family, school and society is a very complex task. We can only suggest some small steps. In this chapter we focus more on what we already have.

1. Preferred Traditional Practices: India has a strong tradition of care of the child and the mother. In fact, the support begins at the foetal stage itself. The mother and the child is a symbiotic unit at least till the time of weaning.

This strong bond is to be nurtured. The developmental stages of childhood are described, well based on observation in all the traditional societies. Hindu tradition calls it *samskaras*. Such rites of passage are part of religions too.

Traditional childcare patterns such as oil massage and baths exist in many traditional societies and these provide excellent stimulation, promoting both physical development and emotional bonding.

2. Play as the key to overall development has been recognised from times immemorial but is being discarded or replaced by gadgets in the recent times, with the advent of technology. Bringing PLAY into the lives of children is essential.

3. Midday Meals for the children have made a huge contribution to nutrition levels and peer relations amongst children. The **R**ight **T**o **E**ducation Act envisages a very bright future for our children. We need to implement the recommendations in earnest.

We generally believe that symptoms are bad things to have and these reveal some illness. But in children, when it comes to understanding symptoms, they lead us to recovery. How do we know when a child needs help?

1. There are **many symptoms** – not just one or two. The more are the symptoms, more severe is the condition. Occasional behavioural problems are common and manageable.
2. If the child is overactive or irritable, sad or tells occasional lies, it is to be considered normal. But if these are **persistent** these need to be attended to.
3. If the problem behaviours are too **frequent** and go on **for a long period** these need to be attended to.
4. **Severity** too matters. Being fearful on occasions is common. But being so fearful that the child refuses to be alone, shows that such a child needs to be helped.

How do we decide that a child needs help? Let us imagine the child has fever. If it is mild you will wait for a few days and then take him to the doctor if it persists. If it is sudden and very high, you will take him to the doctor immediately. Partly the worry that is caused by the fever or the tolerance level of the child or the concern level of the family decides how it is to be responded to, and this determines when he is taken for treatment.

Even with psychological treatment, the same situation holds. It is actually the family that decides when the child needs treatment. When the family is troubled or when the child is in distress or when both occur simultaneously, they consult a doctor. One of the pioneer child psychiatrists, Leo Kanner, in the 1970s spoke of usefulness of symptoms. We paraphrase his words below:

The Symptom in Children

The complaint or the 'symptom' which the patient presents is an indication of the existence of a cause of which it is the effect. The parents bring a child because they are bothered about her/his behaviour; they begin by naming the phenomenon which bothers them and request the clinician to remove the symptom. Experience shows that such limited attention is an ineffective shortcut as it disregards the causes, of which the behaviour item is the effect. The symptom, in addition, also serves a number of important and closely related functions.

The Symptom as an Admission Ticket

The symptom may be looked upon as an admission ticket to the clinician's curiosity. An admission ticket to a playhouse arouses one's curiosity about the play but does not tell one about its contents. A fever may mean several underlying conditions. A physician who treats the fever without looking for its cause falls short of his study. The fever is not the illness; it merely indicates that there is an illness to be investigated. The symptom, thus, is not the problem. It merely indicates that there is a problem to be studied.

A policeman on the beat notices there is a riot. As he cannot cope with the situation alone, he blows his whistle to summon help. The whistle plays the role of a signal which calls attention to the real problem. But the whistle itself is not the problem. Similarly, behaviour problems indicate that there is something bothering the child. Exclusive attention to the whistle or the symptom alone will not serve any purpose. The policeman who blew the whistle knew exactly what his act meant; while the misbehaving child seldom knows what his behaviour means. He does not know what his signal means, or even that he is signaling anything. It is left to the clinician to search for the source of the trouble.

The Symptom as a Safety Valve

Sometimes, behaviours such as stealing or lying are considered as 'bad' behaviour for which the child should be punished and scolded. Often these behaviours are the outcome of severe family pathology. A rebellious child fights the situation while a quiet and obedient child succumbs to severe pathology. The 'bad' behaviour, thus, is a safety valve which allows the child to survive instead of 'drowning'. It is an aggressive defence against powerful forces, with which the child could not possibly cope in a socially accepted manner. It keeps the child's inner resources intact.

The Symptom as a Means of Solving Problems

Sometimes the symptoms solve the problem. A child with difficulties in a new school, which is some distance away, may develop conversion (eg. paralysis of the lower limbs) or dissociative symptoms (eg. fainting spells), and the symptoms keep the child from school, thus offering a solution. The clinician's task is to find an alternative and a better solution than the one the child has opted for.

Many symptoms are of **nuisance value** such as restlessness and fighting. But generally, children with symptoms of nuisance value are brought for treatment by parents and teachers earlier than those children who suffer inwardly. These symptoms may be mismanaged by parents, who themselves have a low threshold for bearing annoyances. For example, sloppiness in a child may not bother one mother at all, while another mother might be driven to punitive behaviour due to her low tolerance or her perfectionism.

In addition, there is a strong cultural element in evaluation of a symptom. In the Indian context, being quiet and obedient is considered as 'model' behaviour and 'talking back' to elders is seen as bad behaviour. Thumb sucking is considered bad behaviour, while over activity in a youngster may be considered as indicator of high intelligence when the child grows older. What is considered normal or abnormal in a particular culture is of crucial importance in all cultures and subcultures, and a clinician must be familiar with the cultural context in which the symptom is reported. Within the same culture, symptoms may become fashionable at different times. A child may use different symptoms as means of communication in different settings.

Family should move away from fixed notions of what the child should be and focus on overall development instead of concentrating only on academic achievement.

No two children are alike in their intellectual or temperamental endowment. In the same home, children who share a common environment, say of parental disharmony with physical aggression: the first child may become very aggressive at school and difficult to manage at home, the second child may become withdrawn, sad and with no interest in school activities. His mind is preoccupied by thoughts of his parents fighting all the time. The third child, however, may escape from the distress and conflict, make friends at school, study well as well as try to help the parents. Their heredity and environment is the same.

How can the three children be so different in their response to their similar environment?

In the West it is described as slow to warm, good or difficult child. The answer lies in the temperament. A Rajasik child reacts with anger, the Tamasik child reacts with sadness of despair while the Satvik child is invulnerable to stress and can even thrive under adversities. Such children are called resilient, they bounce back even when defeated. It is believed that resilient children grow up to be well adjusted and happy, if there is even one single caring adult to support them. So, supporting a child even under dire circumstances go a long way in helping the child. In Indian societies, there are several sources of support for children which strengthen them.

Helpful Factors

- The child has helpful person at home/outside: Somebody whom the child is attached to, who helps the child, takes him out, buys the child gifts.
- The child has friends in the neighbourhood or school.
- The child has interest in drawing, painting, games, music etc.
- The child has many special talents.
- The child is good at sports.
- The child is creative, can put together common place objects in a new fashion, or make objects with hands.

There are many ways in which different people in his world can help him. If such support is given when the child needs it, he makes a smooth transition to a happy adulthood. But being allowed to play is the most natural way of promoting overall development.

Some children are exceptional and gifted. They are characterised by superior verbal ability, reading or doing maths very fast, high curiosity, good memory and recall, keen observation, strong imagination and good problem-solving skills. They are also intensely involved and show persistence in what they do. They also have varied interests and some risk-taking characteristics. It is also possible that they may not fit very well in a normal classroom. They may need different kind of environment.

School

How can we make the school a better place? Obviously, by having better infrastructure and teachers. Infrastructure needs maintenance. Teachers need to upgrade their knowledge. But the most important is that they have to have passion for teaching and care about children. Such teachers are very few.

Change of mindset of teachers to change the way they think about children and to use child-centred play-way method is the only way out. Over the years, I have discovered that lectures, demonstrations and videos are useful. But to change the ways most teachers think of children is hard. Perhaps the only way to persuade them is to demonstrate that their burden will be much reduced by using this method. Also assure them that no time will be taken away from their classes (much as we would like to replace them all together with a child-centred method)!

The teachers believe that one need not give children books, toys, games etc. as they are bound to spoil them. It is a belief among teachers and parents that it is wasteful to give things to children as they destroy it. On the other hand, there are parents who give very expensive objects to children who do not value them. What we need is to give what is optimum – that is a chance to play.

A Programmed Response: Tentative Steps

- 2 weeks (10 sessions of 2 hours duration) of play with children, demonstrated.

- 2 weeks the teachers join in as observers only.
- 2 weeks requesting the teachers and authorities to make available space and time in the last hours of school when everyone is tired or bored. This is the time, child-centred play works the best. But now the programme is managed by children themselves. We have managed to keep the children enjoying, being creative and playing cooperatively. So engrossed they become that they do not want to stop the sessions.

The impact of the programme will be seen in their regular school activities.

Now the programme can be used as a regular feature for all the children every day, as a physical instruction class.

Child-centred play can be used in a variety of settings.

1. For schools where the teacher pupil ratio is poor – such as single teacher primary schools in the rural areas.
2. In slum schools with poor infrastructure and where children come from disadvantaged background.
3. Enhance maths skills and reading English as well as regional languages.
4. It has been used by us with 10-15 sessions to bridge the gap seamlessly between the regular Grade I children and children admitted under the 25% quota to private schools, without pre-schooling. Mostly, these children are discriminated against because they are poor and do not speak English, kept segregated with minimal teaching inputs or humiliated. Even discriminating practices such as wrist bands to show that they are different are used by schools. Many school teachers and authorities have been surprised to find the children exposed to child-centred play, making a smooth transition into Grade I.

5. In places where schools stop functioning or do not exist due to natural or manmade disasters. One can use only whatever available material is there to conduct the programme. It does appear that child-centred play-way method is a panacea. To some extent it is, if it is adopted wholeheartedly by adults who deal with children.
6. The most important aspect is that adults can learn from children what to teach them. There is a quote – every child is a scientist and every scientist is a grown up child!

Society

Now we come to the most difficult part – the society. It is strange that Indian society is so resistant to most liberal ideas and practices but jumps on to a bandwagon to make something totally alien such as mobiles as part of their lives. The dramatic examples are use of television and cell phones! What makes people adapt easily to some ideas and distance themselves from some ideas is too complex to be understood. It is possible for us to adopt the gimmicks used by advertising agencies for the good of human kind.

To Stop

- Abuse and trafficking of children
- Child labour
- Ill treatment in institutions
- Ill treatment in school
- Profiteering in using the children

To Promote

- Safety of children at home, school and outside
- Provide healthy role models
- To promote moral values
- To promote compassion and pro-social behaviour

17

Children of the Forest

A BACKGROUND study of nine tribal residential schools which are called Ashram Schools, led us to explore their homes and community. The tribal colonies were located not too far from the residential schools. Some are government supported, some are only permitted the use of land and some are even on the encroached land.

While most of the studies available in the country consists of demographic data, we looked at health, socio-cultural data and family aspects of these communities. The tribals of HD Kote were originally dwellers of dense expanse of reserve forests straddling Karnataka, Kerala and Tamil Nadu. Building the dam across River Kabini uprooted these tribals. Even today, the rehabilitation efforts are not considered satisfactory by them.

At the time of this study by my team in 2005, they continued to hold traditional values. They spoke their own language and most of the adults were illiterate. In recent years, some boys and girls have gone for higher studies. Traditionally, teenage boys and girls go into a forest and the boy adorns the girl's hair with flower and they come back to the home of the parents as husband and wife! If the marriage does not work out they can choose different partners. They worship forest deities and believe in spirit possessions. In one colony, the parents had created difficult situations with alcoholism and unemployment, it was of no concern to them whether the child went to school or not. But in most of the colonies, they wanted the children in school, when they were not required to work in the farm. We were quite upset when we found that Lakshmi, a very bright girl studying in a class 6, did not come back to the school after summer vacation. Others told us that she went into the forest and married her boy friend!

Among the tribals studied, there were two groups, one called Jenu Kurubas are honey gatherers while the other, Kadu Kurubas are forest dwellers who collect forest produce and sell them. At the time of our study, there was no electricity in those colonies. Consequently, no television or mobiles. These colonies were covered by Primary Health Centres in their area and the hospitals run by the government in the township as well as clinics run by NGOs. Apart from one dysfunctional colony, others had festivals, dances and singing in their languages to keep them entertained. On rare occasions, with the help of generators, movies were shown. Traditional practices of oil massage and bath was given twice a day to the babies.

The prosocial behaviour of the community reflected in the behaviour of children in the ashram schools. Older children took care of the younger children as if they were their own siblings. Their prosocial behaviour was extended to us, once they warmed up to us.

One of the astonishing observation was that among the 800 children studied, there was not a single child with Attention Deficit Hyperactivity Disorder (ADHD). In contrast, in cities the teachers rated 10 out of 100 children as overactive and out of that at least 8 had ADHD. Absence of over activity and attention deficit was because the children grew up with freedom to roam around wherever they liked. They were never restrained from running around, playing in mud, climbing trees and freely indulging in all kinds of activities, even without supervision in another part of the village.

In June of 2004, when we went visiting nine schools, these were at three different directions 20 to 30 kms away from the headquarters, it took us three days to visit the Ashram schools.

When we began working, no matter how many children were there, there were only one or two teachers. Subsequently NGOs hired 50 local youngsters to help the school. Though enthusiastic, they had very low pay Rs 5,000 per month and no job security as these were contract jobs.

The interventions with the help of our field staff were carried out for 800 children. Four teacher training workshops were held. As many as 510 children were tested before and after the intervention. The interventions were carried out in a staggered manner over 20 to 25 sessions.

About 52.36 per cent were boys and 47.63 per cent were girls at these schools from class 1 to 7. The ratio was fairly satisfactory.

Tests administered were to assess attention, intelligence, memory, arithmetic, vocabulary and creativity. Age trends showed improvement of baselines, while pre-post assessments showed significant improvement on all the parameter. The assessments showed that in both the groups boys and girls improved significantly on all the tests. In the Seguin Form Board Test,*[7] time taken had reduced dramatically indicating higher IQ status.

On the simple and complex attention tasks, the boys and girls had similar attention spans and memory skills. On the speed of performance in the intelligence test, the boys had a higher baseline performance. This is hard to explain. Their arithmetic and vocabulary scores were similar.

On all parameters there was significant improvement in both the groups. Interestingly the girls outperformed boys at the baseline level. Their performance was similar to the boys in the intelligence test, unlike in the younger children on creativity tests, where both groups started similarly but in baseline studies, the boys outperformed girls.

However, it must be pointed out on tests of intelligence, the baseline performance **across age** was very poor, at the lower percentiles of 10th and below. On post programme assessment, almost all the children reached the average and some even above the average level. **This indicates the fallacy of using standard Western tests to assess the children from first generation literates, be it in urban, rural or tribal schools.**

There is a view point that the IQ measured in a test standardised on a population belonging to another culture does not give accurate results. The test which was used, Raven's Progressive Matrices, is considered culture free or culture fair test, which obviously it is not.

Because of the unfamiliarity with complex designs, colours and numbers, we used tests which are very simple for children

---

[7] The Seguin Form Board Test is based on the single factor theory of intelligence, measures speed and accuracy. It is useful in evaluating a child's eye-hand coordination and form perception.

of class one and two. We used a sheet with coloured dots instead of numbers or letters of the alphabet. For assessment of intelligence, a simple form board (Seguin Form Board) test was used. Mehdi's tests of creativity was used. Vocabulary and number work was assessed. Class 1 and 2 had Seguin Form Board tests as the test of intelligence, while classes 3 to 7 had Raven's Progressive Matrices as test of intelligence. Seguin Form Board scores indicated more time was needed to complete the tests.

When I started working in these schools, I had heard the expression by the teachers 'the untouchables are unteachable!' My experience with the tribal children was totally opposite to what was believed by the teachers, before we started on the programme.

The children were very friendly and pro-social, very creative and innovative in all the activities they were asked to imitate and carry out, very dexterous in making objects from odds and ends. So much so, these children went to Talent Shows in Taluk Headquarters and brought back prizes, which they joyfully displayed. What a contrast to the shy and fearful children turning out to be happy and bright children!

The unusual **prosocial behaviour** which I have not seen in urban or rural government schools may be due to the following reasons:

1. Spirit of community living pervades in these colonies. They all depend on each other for support.
2. Freedom to play and wander around anywhere and anytime.
3. Absence of television which mainly shows programmes which have aggressive content.
4. Leisurely pace of life, despite poverty and hardships, deep faith in gods and rituals, in general old ways of living.

Jerome Kagan has recently condemned ADHD as an artifact promoted by the pharmaceutical industry and collusion of teachers and parents in creating an enabling environment for **promoting hyperactivity** and **labelling** it as a disorder that needs treatment.

The tribal children whom I saw a decade ago indicates that ADHD is a product of modern civilisation. But now the situation may have changed with the advent of television and mobiles in the same communities. This would be an interesting research for exploration and may be taken up by a group of mental health experts in Mysore.

Can we save some of these preferred practices for posterity?

1. Massage and oil bath for infants, babies and nursing mothers. (These soothe the child as well as enhance the muscle tone/coordination.)
2. Encourage cooperative and empathic behaviour.
3. When audio visual inputs are given, these need to be screened for unhealthy role model behaviour as children are excellent mimics.
4. Child-centered play is the best way to promote these desirable characteristics.

I would like to highlight an extremely negative aspect of teachers. I told them that there are four kinds of aggression manifested in schools. This was described by the World Health Organisation.

1. Aggression of the teacher against the child.
2. Aggression of one child against the other.
3. Aggression against objects in the schools.
4. Aggression against the teacher.

The teachers as a group sheepishly reported that they were aggressive against children but the children **did not show any**

aggression against objects, other children or the teachers. If children did not show any aggression, why were the teachers punishing them? This menace has a large presence across the country. This needs to be condemned and stopped.

18

Promotion of Psychosocial Development*

'IF CHILDREN should not play – who else should?' We often ask the parents and the teachers who bring the children for consultation in our clinic. *In India there is a popular misconception that play is a waste of time and the time is better spent studying!*

Play is the most powerful tool, which enables the child to achieve overall normal development without the domineering pressure of the adults. The fact that even a young child can create and learn from his/her environment through play has had strong support from the current research in developmental psychology.

This chapter can be considered a school manual and is based on our experience of work with 1,200 rural school children

---

* The authors of the chapter are Malavika Kapur and Uma H.

and 800 tribal school children. The worksheets can be in any language and so can the interactions.

The manual aims at sensitising the people who work with children such as teachers in urban and rural government schools, those who work with children at risk such as street children, those in orphanages, those exposed to and affected by natural/manmade disasters, by physical or psychological abuse, and by HIV/AIDS or chronic physical illness. In summary, the adults who deal with children who suffer and are deprived of normal childhood can use the manual.

The deprivation comes in the way of normal development. The adults need to be sensitive and provide an environment, which heals and promotes normal psychosocial development. The play-away methods suggested in this manual fulfil this function.

However, these programmes can be carried out effectively only if it has the wholehearted support of the people in charge such as education, social welfare and health authorities. The cooperation of the staff involved in the programme should be enlisted. The workers themselves are motivated through demonstration (live or video) of the impact of the intervention and actual hands-on experience and being appreciated for their work. Minor incentives such as money for travel, small honorarium, meals, certificates go a long way in motivating, especially when the work is voluntary.

It was found that using the methods described in this manual over 20 to 25 sessions, one hour a day and six days a week, the children showed significant improvement on psychological tests which were administered before and after the intervention.

The improvements occurred in the following areas though the traditional teaching methods were not used and only the child-friendly play-away methods were used:

Attention
Memory
Intelligence
Creativity
Vocabulary
Arithmetic
How did we work with the children?
Following are some observations:

We Respect the Children as Individuals

We Do Not Instruct or Teach (We help, provide the material, time and space in the schools).

The activities were initiated by us and unobtrusively supervised. We played the role of catalysts rather than instructors. The programmes were expanded and refined by the children themselves.

Find out What the Children Already Know

These could be games, songs, dances or stories. They may have learnt these from other children, the teachers, their families or their community.

Warming Up

Warming up activities to break the ice is absolutely essential.

The rural children, even more so the tribal children, are shy and fearful of their teachers and strangers. Quite understandably so in the schools where the STICK is the main teaching aid, as the teachers punish them in the name of discipline. In each of the sections some warming up activities are described.

We always applaud, praise and encourage and ask the children to do the same. No matter what the child creates it is praise worthy.

We Never Criticize or Make Fun!

Domains of Development

The programme aims at enhancing the development in the following areas to lesser to greater extent:

Motor
Intellectual
Language
Emotional
Social
Moral
Sexual

Description of the Activities

The activities carried out fall into the following categories with some overlap amongst them. These will be described in detail in the following section. These were:

Artwork
Craftwork
Songs and dances
Language, games and dramas
Arithmetic exercises
Life skills and role-play

Basic Kit

The Basic Kits for the schools had different components namely, for an individual child, for a group of children and the entire school.

- For each child, a drawing book, a slate (for younger children), pencils, crayons, colour pencils or water colours and stationery or craft material or newspapers.
- Beads, blocks and foam beads of different colours, shapes and sizes.
- For the groups, KG Card boards, paints and brushes, Kolata sticks and bronze anklets, tambourines and cymbals for dances.

Indoor games are the board games such as carrom, draughts, ludo, snakes and ladders and chess and some traditional board games made locally. Outdoor games are like tennycoit, badminton, cricket, football and volleyball.

Instructional material such as Chinese abacus and simple graded books depicting stories with themes familiar to the children were used. It is estimated that the basic kit containing the above could be provided at about approximately Rs 10,000 per school and later on about Rs 2,000-3,000 per year, to replenish the material each year. This is not a big investment considering the gains.

The following section gives a descriptive account of the activities and their possible contribution to the enhancement of various domains of development. It was possible to assess the gains in attention, memory, intelligence, creativity, language and arithmetic skills in an objective manner, it was not possible to do so in the areas of emotional, social, moral, sexual development. But the activities in general aimed at promoting all the areas.

Songs and Dances

We started with what they already know. We encouraged them to use the Kolata sticks, bronze ghungroos and tambourines. Children love these accompaniments. These songs and dances are of different kinds.

Some songs and dances taught by the teachers. These are often moral tales. For example, there is a dance of a sparrow seeking refuge from the trees in a storm. The trees, which refuse to give shelter, are destroyed in the storm. It is the tree that gives the shelter that sways and bends but survives the storm.

Some songs and dances are from the movies. The children mimic these film sequences very well, including the 'break dance' sequences – which are very popular. The songs and dances were also learnt from their own people. These are often sung in distinct languages and dialects of their own with unique dance steps. For example, the Lambanis (Marathi-speaking gypsy like population) have graceful dances with songs, welcoming the outsiders by incorporating their names into the songs. There are songs and dances depicting the agricultural work of sowing, weeding, harvesting, winnowing the grains and so on.

In one of the schools, two children sang and danced a romantic theme. The young man is trying to placate his beloved who is sulking. It goes like this: 'Come with me – I will give you flowers for your hair.' She continues to sulk, he wipes her tears. 'Come with me, I will give you silver anklets.' 'Come with me, I will give you ear rings.' 'Come with me, I will give you a new saree.' Each time she rebuffs him saying she did not get anything from his earlier promises as she continues to weep. Finally, he says, 'Okay, if that is how you feel, I will find a new girl!' Immediately the girl coyly agrees for reconciliation. The theme depicts the reality. Till the last line, one gets the impression that she is an empowered woman, and the last line depicts the stark reality.

Warming Up

We generally found the children stiff, fearful and quiet. We would ask one of the children, whoever volunteered first, to show a daily activity. For example:

- Washing the face
- Brushing the teeth
- Combing the hair
- Braiding the hair
- Washing the dishes
- Washing clothes
- Going to school

This goes on until all the children in the group show the various daily activities. Then we ask them to convert these into dance actions. Then each activity is converted into a common dance action. Then they are asked to speed up the dance actions, one after the other. As a last step each child in the groups follows his original dance sequence in the group dance. This is a very popular warm up exercise.

In fact, one of the children was crying out of fear when we started the activity. We asked him and a friend to make it into an activity and incorporated into the dance sequence. When the boy danced the crying action, all of them burst into laughter and so did he. Whenever we went around the school video recording, boys and girls, younger and older, would dance tirelessly unwilling to stop, so that their dances are recorded. Somehow, dancing and singing seem to be an antidote for shyness and fear.

Developmental Domains in Songs and Dances

i. Skills of movements
ii. Rhythm in movements and sounds
iii. Overcoming shyness and fear
iv. Expression of thoughts and feelings
v. Learning by imitation

Artwork

The aim of the artwork practised by us is not to promote artistic or aesthetic skills. It may incidentally happen along the way. We try to communicate to the children that all of them can draw and paint, whatever they like and in the manner, they wish to. There are no set rules or standards. At this stage the children are anxious. They hesitate to start. They try to copy designs on the water colour or crayon box, or some picture around or draw 'rangoli' or national flag, which they are taught. Copying has to be discouraged. The child is helped to relax with the following exercises.

Warming Up Some simple exercises are given

Warming Up. Some simple exercises, are given.

- Make a small squiggle on the black board or on a sheet of paper and ask the child to draw something from it and make it elaborate. For example, a 's' squiggle be made into a snake or a peacock by a child.
- Colour a thread and place it on a paper and fold it. When the paper is opened there is design on it. The child can be asked to draw extra lines and make it elaborate.
- Take a flower or a leaf, colour it and press it on the paper. Even thumb impressions can be the starting point.
- Make a ribbon of the leaf or flower, by keeping the paper on it and scratching with a pencil.
- Draw a theme such as yourself, your family, your school, festivals, what you like best and so on.

The child becomes more relaxed and starts to explore the lines and colours in a free manner. Usually children enjoy these activities in each other's company and learn from them.

We used different formats for artwork.

Drawing Book

Each child is given a drawing book and a box of crayons. First his/her name is written on it. Then he is asked to start on the first page and draw whatever he/she likes. But the child is allowed one page, once a week, for the entire year! Surprisingly the children appreciated this personal possession so much that they used the single drawing box and book slowly, methodically and over several months. The crayon box was intact, with the crayons being used carefully, not broken or lost like we find with children who have abundance of art supplies.

KG Card Board

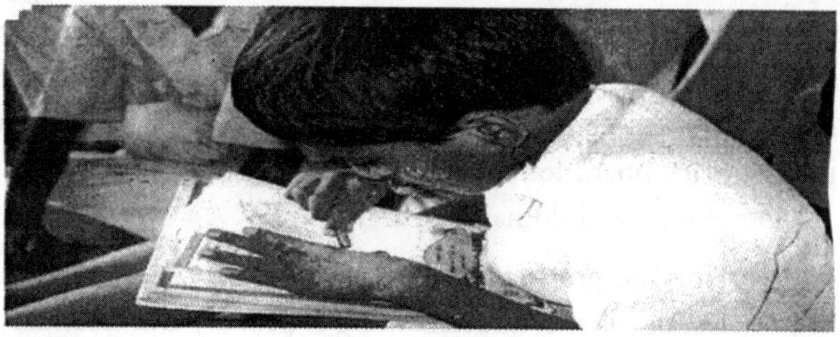

A cardboard sheet is given to a group of four children to work together on a theme. Younger children use crayons or pencils. Older ones can use water colours or poster colours. This enables them to work cooperatively and explore themes such as draw or paint 'your village', 'your school' or 'forest' and so on.

Large sheets of papers to be used as wall murals. We use 'rangoli powder', preferably vegetable dyes, which are inexpensive and can be bought in bulk. The powders are mixed separately in small containers with gum and water.

Brushes can be brought or even made with locally available grass or coconut fronds. If you have a space about 4 feet high and 10 feet long, 10 children can share the space and create a mural. Each child is allotted one-foot space. We have witnessed most attractive, colourful murals depicting the grand display of flora and fauna of the area.

We have also seen children expressing their emotions in their artwork. For example, a girl who had lost her father recently drew an unusual creature, which she called a spirit. Amongst the tribals they have a belief that dead person's spirit hovers around for 12 days before going to heaven or hell.

But mostly the pictures are joyous and colourful. If there are no papers or colours, old newspapers too can be used instead. Colours can be prepared from clay, leaves and flowers, which are found around the school. Children were found to be exceedingly creative in preparing the colours and the brush. You simply have to say, 'what are the colours you can make?' Can you make a large or a small brush to use with the colours? One can even use the black board for some of the drawing exercises.

Developmental domains in artwork:

- Fine and gross motor skills
- Use of colours: understanding of primary and secondary colours
- Expression and Communication of emotions, reality, fantasy, creativity and aesthetics
- Increase in dexterity depending on the medium used i.e. pencils, crayons or paints
- Crayons are easier to handle while and brush and colours are the most difficult

Do not say, 'Is this a car? A tree?' The children may have drawn or painted something quite different. When you ask questions such as these, the children feel threatened or humiliated. They think that they should draw what you expect them to.

Always ask the children to discuss what they have drawn. Pick the art product and show them to the other children. Get them to appreciate the artwork of other children. Gently dissuade them from being critical.

Try and display as many art products as possible in the classroom. Allow the children take some home to show to the parents and keep with them. If the children are asked to copy a design, as usually practised by drawing masters, they all draw the same thing—a table, a bunch of grapes or a flower. If they are asked draw on their own a flower, an animal, a tree or a person they draw it out of their imagination. Hence no art product is alike in a free art session.

Each child may draw sometimes even recognisable forms uniquely. Young children tend to draw themselves as bigger figures than the adults around! Children's drawing evolves slowly from simple to complex representations across ages.

Craft Work

Making various objects with paper, leaves and other objects found in the environment was an activity that the children enjoyed a great deal.

They were not instructed in how to make anything. Traditionally, craft instruction means that the instructor demonstrates how things are made like crape paper flowers or 'origami' kind of designs with paper. We simply provided the children with papers. Coloured papers or even newspapers along with scissors – we asked the children to the papers into any shapes as they were or when they were folded. Each child would cut and make his or her own designs. Then they would experiment with more complex design – fold the papers in anyway they liked and make different objects. For example, invariably one child would know how to make a boat or a cap. In one of the groups of 12-year-olds, they were able to make forty different objects in about 30 minutes. These were aeroplane, arrows, hat, boat, ship, canoe, inkpot, sunglasses, shirt, dress, and many children holding hands, windmill and so on.

- Similarly, coconut palm leaves were proved to be versatile medium. Children on their own made snakes, watches, sunglasses and even parrots. They would use broomsticks to join the pieces together into even more elaborate objects.
- They would cut, or fold KG Card boards to make flags, ships, crowns, etc. One can even make moving vehicle and other objects with sticks, leaves and berries.
- They would make collages using grains, berries, sticks and flowers and colours.

- They would make objects, which work as whistles, flutes, drums and string instruments and telephones using two tins.

Appreciation of their efforts is the key to the success of the programmes. **It is important after these activities** tidying up the workspace and putting away the things neatly is an important aspect of these activities. Please display the products in the classroom.

Domains of activity provided by craftwork:

- Fine motor and gross motor skills
- Visuo-spatial perceptual skills
- Visuo-motor coordination skills
- Understanding of textures, thickness, flexibility of the materials and the appropriate uses
- Creativity
- Ability to imitate activities and learn from others

Language Games

Since we had earlier discovered that the children were very reluctant to speak in the classroom and to the teachers and their vocabulary seemed very limited, we had a large number of activities to enhance speech and language including reading, writing and comprehension functions. We also saw a clear relationship between language functions, intelligence, memory and creativity. They ranged from very simple to very elaborate games.

Warming Up

Word Games

Initially very simple exercises were used such as name an animal, a bird, a flower, a colour etc.

Then to name a group of certain objects under a particular category, food or furniture. For example, Table, Bench, Chair.

Similarities and dissimilarities between two objects such as a stone and a mango.

Following these exercises, when children tended to relax, we introduced slightly more complex word games. In addition, picture and word matching and looking at maps, picture of animals, plants were used to enhance the vocabulary. Name an object starting with letter Aa or Ee, Name animals or flower starting with the letter Aa or Ee. Name an object, which begins with the last syllable of the word given by a child. The common game of *Anthakshari* was thus introduced.

Then we would have two teams competing. Two children who have good handwriting will enter the responses of the A and B teams. Now the words are to be provided by each team to the specific instruction. At times, the winning team would come up quickly with 20-30 words in a very short time. When the games become easy, children made them more difficult by introducing difficult words and new rules. Children not only engaged in the games, their vocabulary improved at a very rapid pace, even by listening to the others play, even while not participating themselves.

Sentence Games

- Given a word, the child should make a sentence using it.
- Describe objects in the environment, animals, trees and their uses.
- These were converted into team games where elaborate and complex sentences were given higher scores.
- Description of an event followed by the sounds. For example, the rainfall—tap, tap, tap. The coconut falls........... The thunder goes...................
- What is big? What is small?

Cow – Calf

Sentences to promote clear speech such as sentences with syllable repetition were introduced. Two examples are in Kannada—about the tank bund in 'Tarikere'—in which 'tari' and 'kere' gets repeated continuously—in a tongue twister sequence. The next one goes like this: The old man from Tarikere comes to the market on the shady day. His wife, wife's uncle, uncle's daughter, daughter's husband, husband's sister, sister's dog, dog's tail and the tip of the tail come to the market. The children are expected to repeat it in the right sequence without stopping at a high speed.

Story Telling and Story Construction

The stories were of different kinds.

- Stories from *Panchatantra*, *Jataka* or from the epics *Ramayana* or *Mahabharatha*.
- Stories, which are a takeoff on a popular story given above.
- Stories about animals and forest deities and local lores —told by their elders.

- Newly made up stories by the children using their own imagination.

These stories could be what they had heard from the teachers, other children or their families. Some children could make up stories, which were very elaborate, and these children were admired a great deal by the others.

Children were asked to make up stories where one child begins a story. After the first sentence another child provides the next sentence. Initially the children were hesitant, and the stories had tame beginning, middle and end. But as time went on they were able to build interesting and complicated stories.

Find Out and List Out What the Children Already Know

Riddles and Proverbs

These were veritable storehouse of children's language skills and abstraction. Children simply loved them, and learnt the new ones very quickly, as the discussion went on about the meanings and the answers. As many of the riddles were on 'dirty' topics such as 'snot', children were amused no end. But these proverbs and riddles covered almost every object in their environment and were very culture specific. A content analysis of the riddles and proverbs would be an interesting exercise. The following are the translations of some of the riddles and proverbs we had collected. Of course, these do not translate well.

Riddles

1. The rice that cannot be washed. Or the mat that cannot be folded (stars and sky). There are several variations to this.
2. Ploughed field has a snake on it (rope). There are several variations to this.
3. On a tree several leaves speak (harmonium).

4. Floats, sinks, melts (paan or betel leaf, betel nut and slaked lime).
5. Orphan child but cannot be caught (water).
6. Lamp is lit on the mountain (nose ring).
7. Short guy weaves the fence (needle and thread).
8. Roars in the corner (raagi grinding stone).
9. Jeep goes in a dish (snot).
10. Green outside, white inside (radish).
11. It is in the field, has nine doorways (anthill).
12. Green doctor, red patients, black tablets (watermelon). There are several variations to this.
13. Inside the red box, anklets making 'gili-gili' sounds (red chillies).
14. Linganna, Ninganna, remove the cloths and swallow Brothers! (banana).
15. A bud when inside, blooms when outside (umbrella).
16. One hit - a house full of children (garlic).
17. All around coconut trees – in between lies water (eye lashes).
18. On the mountain – tree, on the tree - flowers, on the flowers – the berry (chilli).
19. One-eyed man has one eye. The baby has three eyes (coconut).
20. If you pluck it does not dry up, if you plant it, does not grow (hair).
21. The pond is full of foot marks of the sheep (stars). There are several variations to this.
22. Above the well, parrot, above the parrot, a maidan, above the maidan, forest (face, mouth, nose, forehead and hair).
23. Born in water, grows in water and dies in water (salt).
24. House full of flowers (dew drops).

25. Moon has only one sister (bunch of banana).
26. The house has only one pillar (umbrella).
27. White cow above which black cow (urad seed).
28. Tiny girl has long braid (needle and thread).
29. White man has a black cap (matchstick.)
30. Younger sister can go into elder sister's house, but the elder sister cannot go into younger sister (Seru and Paavu – units of measuring of grains, seer and paav).
31. Over the roof, the 'mandi', above it is the temple of 'Mahadeshwara', on the top sits 'Ayyappa' (honey in the beehive).
32. There is water in the well, and there is silver in the water (lamp).
33. Appajappa's garden is locked with a lock costing 70 rupees. No one can open it (death).
34. Surrounded by white washed wall. No door way (egg).
35. One jar has two kinds of oil (egg).
36. It is green, but it is not a parrot, it has a top knot (Shikha) but not Narada, but has three eyes, but not Shiva, it has water, but is not a well (tender coconut).

Proverbs

1. One who has no worry can sleep in the market place.
2. Sing and sing you have a 'Raaga', groan and groan you have 'Roga' (disease).
3. After Tugar, the crops decline, after birth of the babies' strength decline.
4. One who lives in harmony with others has heavenly happiness.
5. Where there is mind, there is a way.
6. Don't feed the one who had a meal, don't oil the head which has no hair.
7. Stretch your legs as far as the mattress.

8. One who eats without work, even a large pot of gold will not last.
9. Snakes does not die, stick does not break.
10. Hand in soil (mud), curds in mouth.
11. Good people's company is sweet as honey.
12. Daughter is like the mother, thread is like the saree.
13. One who bears may last.
14. King to the land, but son to the mother.
15. Ruby in monkey's hand.
16. Truth is immortal, lie is endless.
17. Nothing tastier than salt. No chosen relative than mother.
18. If the plant does not bend, will it bend as a tree?
19. Full water pot does not spill.

Collect all the RIDDLES and the PROVERBS that children already know and discuss their meaning and ask them to create new ones. Make notebook in which they are listed and ask them to keep adding new ones whenever they think of them.

We learn from this exercise that **Riddles** employ commonplace objects and events. Description of the rural environment, which consists of farmland, crops, plants, trees commonly found. The agricultural focus cannot be missed in the descriptions though they are simple and not very sophisticated. Some of them even appear more recent in origin. The **Proverbs** on the other hand appear to have a larger common base with the rest of the country. These are sayings, which have been in existence probably in all the regions.

It is interesting to examine the local contexts in the riddles and common contexts in the proverbs from an anthropological perspective. What is of interest to us is the abundance of both riddles and proverbs in the children in their day-to-day communication indicating a rich language heritage.

In a similar manner, we have rich collection of their stories and songs. It was noted that initially the children were very stiff and formal. They were encouraged to speak, narrate and describe using gestures and action. Gradually they learned to relax and use speech and gesture as normal communication. They were even encouraged to enact the stories, which they did in a most creative manner.

Reading

Most of the children had very poor reading skills. The conventional teaching of reading consisted of the following steps, especially for Kannada, which was the medium of instruction. All the Indian languages, including Kannada are phonetic languages. It is required that the child learns the script first – before learning to read. The child has to learn:

The letters vowels and consonants, which is 13 X 5 X 10 = 650 individual letters. In addition, there are accents and half letters. It is an elaborate and complex system. No teacher recognises the fact that the phonetic scripts are the hardest to read and write for a young child. Copying these elaborate letter structures requires:

- Fine motor skills
- Visuo-spatial perception and discrimination between the letters
- Recognising the shape and linking the sound of the syllables

The above tasks are obviously very difficult and at the same time meaningless and tediously boring. **Our approach to reading is entirely opposed to the traditional approach.** We believe that children love to hear stories. If they are read stories to – they enjoy it equally. If there are pictures, they enjoy it even more.

When the child understands that the entry into the world of stories can also be through BOOKS instead of a PERSON, it is a great revelation. The transition between enjoying listening to a story and reading story is a smooth one, and comes in an **enjoyable effortless** manner. The entry into the world of books is a joyous one.

So, we adopted a different approach to reading. We used a 'top down' approach to reading – adopted for adult literacy programmes of the UNESCO in Mysore in the early 1950s by Shivarama Karanth, a noted author in Kannada. He had prepared primers in Kannada, with illustration with simple stories with words of graded difficulty level. There were two books about a village suffering from draught and how a wandering ascetic influenced the villagers to change it into a prosperous village. There were also simple stories from the epic Ramayana.

We photocopied these books into large copies, which can be seen from a distance of 10 feet by all the children in a class. The steps in promoting reading were:

- Read the entire story aloud – word by word, sentence by sentence, page by page running the finger below each word while reading and also pointing to the picture.
- After one reading, the reader would ask the children to repeat after him, as he read the story following the same sequence as before.
- After 3 or 4 readings, questions are asked to find out whether the children had understood the events and sequences in the story.
- This would go on for several sessions until all the children could read the story by rote. It is very natural for children to enjoy a story, however number of times they are repeated. Unlike adults they do not tire of listening to the same stories.

- Now comes a stage, rather imperceptibly when the child starts recognising the key words, and later the rest of them though the differences in the shapes and formation of the letters. Suddenly the child becomes a reader. This is when he or she asks for more books to read.
- When you have a child, who is already a reader or has become a reader during this exercise, you can ask him to read to the other children. If you do not believe that children can become skilled readers through these methods, **please try it yourself with a group of non-readers!**

We have had many groups of children, an older child or a good reader goes over the repeated exercises of reading this primer called, *Jogi Kanda Ooru* or *The village that the Ascetic saw.*

In one school, we saw a very elaborate enactment of *Jogi Kanda Ooru.*

All our children have become excellent readers by adopting this method. We believe that once the reading skills are acquired and the fine motor and gross motor skills are acquired though play, art and craft activities around the age of 8-10, copying letters becomes an easy task. **Reading Should Come First. Writing May Be Introduced Much Later.**

Continuing with language skills we move on to another activity.

Drama and Skits

We start with a simple warming up story and drama. This is a story about a boy who was very dirty. He was called Hesi (Dirty) Gundanna. He did not like to wash his face, brush his teeth, bathe or change clothes. He did not even like to go to the school. One morning he went out to play instead of going to school. He met the other children going to school. He called out,'come and play with me'. They said, 'you are dirty, we won't play with you – and we are going to school'. He went further on and found a cat, then a dog, and then a cow and so on and all the animals refused to play with him. Finally, he meets a pig playing in a filthy ditch and it calls him and says,'Gundanna – come and play with me'. Totally ashamed of himself, Gundanna rushes home, gets ready to go to school. Now, everyone wants his company.

We ask the children to play the various roles in the story. Slowly they start dramatising and enjoying the story. This is particularly suited for younger children. Initially they may take time to warm and require some prompting and encouragement to act the story out. This is an excellent story to drive home the fact about personal hygiene, especially as most tribal children who come from their homes are unwashed and unkempt.

In another school, they enacted the story of Bandit Veerappan – impromptu. A boy simply touched the blackboard with his finger to gather chalk dust and drew swirling huge moustache above his lips and on the cheeks, the trademark of the bandit.

In another school the boys dramatised a sequence very beautifully about a man getting possessed by a female deity and the devotee asking for blessings and prophecies. The teachers were astounded by the slickness of the production! We told the teachers, you do not need to teach children to put up a play. This is the proof that they can do it on their own. Our greatest reward was at the end of the year, many children in several of the schools improved their native skills dramatically.

Domains of Development Enhanced by the Language and Dramatic Activities

- Enhancement of vocabulary and speech (oral).

- Abstract thinking related to similarities, size, textures, colours, objects.
- Problem solving and abstraction through riddles and proverbs.
- Verbal facility and quick reaction time.
- Problem solving.
- Exercises in speed and clear articulation.
- Creativity and imagination through storytelling, enactment, speaking, extempore.
- Reading skills through the 'top down' method.

Sports, Games and Play

Material for sports, indoor and outdoor games were provided to all the schools, in addition to the stationery, pencils and crayons. The supply of the material made us very popular and was appreciated by the children, parents and teachers alike. Most schools were poorly supplied with sports and games materials and these were not replenished when they were old or damaged or parts got lost.

In general, the teachers did not allow the children to play, even when they could not attend to them. As a rule, they did not want the children to be boisterous and noisy. They wanted them to sit quietly and learn things by rote or copy from the black boards or books. If the children played on their own, it was acceptable at lunch breaks. Whenever they became noisy, the teacher would come with a stick and hit them.

In one of our earliest experience in one of the schools in the Matkere area, we learnt our lesson about how to teach children how to play! We had gone to a school at noontime. It was the lunch break. We had unloaded the sports and games material and had handed over the tennicoit rings to the children when the bell rang. We too went off to have our picnic lunch under a tree offering us shade.

When we came back after an hour, the children were already playing with the rings. Then they demonstrated to us ten different ways in which tennicoit rings can be used – each being an equally interesting method and as good as the original rules. If the equipment can be used in different ways, why not? After all, a ball too can be used in so many different ways.

It is worthwhile remembering some basic equipment can be used for a wide range of games. For example, a small soft ball, a small hard ball, a large football can be used for different games. Often children can think of new ways of using these materials. Multiple uses of objects should be encouraged.

Following this experience, we became more flexible in the instructions, often letting children lead the way and explain their games. The children were very quick to grasp the rules of the game. In fact, in one of the school, 5th graders were playing the chess game and even teaching their teachers how to play the game.

In addition to the formal games, we also attempted to observe and record the details of the games the children already knew and played. To our surprise we gathered a long list of games! We found that some games were common all over India. We also found the tribal children had the maximum number of games and their variations compared to the other rural children.

Some Common Games

Find Out What Games the Children Already Know

1. Lagori/Pitthu

Two teams of five children each play this game. One group builds a tower-like structure using seven stones or wooden pieces. The other group throws a ball to topple it from a stipulated distance. If they don't hit the tower they are considered defeated and have to play again. The team that rebuilds the tower is considered

the winning team. It is important not to get hit by the rival team while rebuilding the tower.

2. Marbles/Gulli-danda

Children may play the game in twos and see that the marble reaches a previously marked spot, in least number of shots. Winner gets the marbles and the loser loses them. It requires great finger dexterity and precision to win.

3. Cap Game

One child plays the cap seller and others sit in a circle facing each other. The cap seller shouts, 'Who wants to buy caps?' They ask, 'What cap?' He says,'Gold Cap'. They ask, 'How much does it cost?' He says,'Thousand rupees!' Then they bend and pretend they are paying the money. At that time, the cap seller quietly keeps the cap behind one of the children. If the child catches him in the act, he loses and has to become a seller again. If the child is caught unawares, he loses and become the cap seller. The game goes on like this.

4. The Lake and the Bank

This has several variations like ocean and beach, river and bank and so on. A large circle is drawn. About 20 to 30 children stand outside it. One child announces either 'lake' or 'bank'. When the word 'bank' is heard, they have to be outside the circle and when it is 'lake' they have to be inside. They have to keep jumping in and out quickly. The announcer mixes up and repeats the sequences. Each child who makes mistake is out of the game. The winner is the one who makes no mistake when the game ends.

5. Tiger and the Cow Game

As many as 30-40 children hold hands and make a protective circle. A child, who is a good runner, is the tiger and is outside the circle. The child who is the cow is inside the circle and is protected by the rest of the children. The tiger has to isolate the cow away from the protectors and catch it. The tiger asks the children whether the cow is there and they say 'No!' The tiger is not allowed into the circle, the tiger wins the game when he captures the cow.

6. Train Game

One child becomes an engine and rest of the children become the bogies. The engine moves and the rest have to follow making Chug-Chug noises without a break.

7. Hide and Seek

There are variations in the singsong manner in which the one that seeks calls out. Many local versions of the calls are created. The word 'I Spy' has been converted into strange sounding words in the various Indian languages.

8. Blind Man's Bluff

There is again local variation of the game.

9. Hopscotch

Different types of this game are popular among the village children.

10. Musical Chair and Its Local Variations

11. There are popular team games, which promote colour and number concepts.

12. Games with two teams. These are cricket, football, volleyball, badminton and the two Indian games, Khokho for the girls and Kabaddi for the boys, which they play.

The tribal children in our sample gave us description of 57 games! There are large numbers amongst them which are the variations of a major games described above.

- There are games of getting an object that is being guarded without being caught.
- Many of them attempt to facilitate quick reaction and response time to instructions like with two sets of activities, only one of which is to be obeyed. The variations for example 'drink coffee or look at the mirror', 'pick the nut or remove the weed', 'gourd or pumpkin', 'change or exchange'.
- An increase in the difficulty level is introduced when you have to show the opposite action when you hear the word 'vada-drink pyasa'.
- There are games where a handicap is introduced – when one has to hop, race, catch all on one leg or blind folded, or with frog like movements.

Domains of development enhanced through the games and play.

- Reaction time speeded up
- Response time speeded up
- Quick response to compeer instruction
- Fine motor and gross motor skill enhancement
- Visuo-motor coordination
- Physical ability and coordination
- Kinaesthetic skill enhancement
- Team games involving following rules–social codes and even ethical codes
- Games as chess and draughts involve complicated planning and problem solving
- Relaxation and energy deployment

Number Games

- Number games involve imitating or clapping hands according to instructions, forming into small groups to the exact number called out, etc.

- The numbers can be taught concretely using matchsticks, broomsticks (separately and in bundles, cowries, beads or pods) to be counted and grouped.
- Shopkeeper and customers – transacting paper money.
- Rhymes describing numbers.
- Reading a clock.
- Bringing specified number of objects from around.
- Match numbers on the cards and sticks.
- Mental sum games and games like,'10 yellow laddoos in a dish –Ambujaate one – how many are left?'

Our main tool of teaching addition, subtraction, division and multiplication in 'ones', 'tens', 'hundreds' and 'thousands' was the Chinese abacus. The children learn the basic arithmetic skills very quickly on the abacus. The Chinese abacus has thirteen columns with a middle line. Below are columns of five beads and above two beads. We got the toy makers of the Channapatna (famous for toque work toys) to manufacture the ABACUS for us. We gave two-three abacuses to each school.

Life Skills

We got a group of 10-12 children to enact a situation common in their area. There is one Coracle boat[8] which can take only 10 people. The boatman or the other passengers have to be persuaded to take an extra person. Here each person responds in a different way. The children interchange the roles. At the end, the best way of conflict resolution and negotiation is highlighted.

Role-play: The children enact conflict situations, playing key participants. Once again everybody discusses how it could have been done better. When refused a school trip by the parents,

---

[8] A large bamboo strips basket covered by buffaloe skin (now plastic sheets are used).

while boys fight, the girls sulk and go off food. Girls fail to negotiate with the family to go for further studies. We get the children to role-play how they would negotiate with the teachers and parents and get across their points of view.

Story and Discussion

For example, an ancient traditional story is told. Here a married young woman is left behind by her husband with his mother and sister. The woman develops a relationship with a young man. She swims to meet him, holding on to an earthen pot everyday. One day her mother-in-law finds out about her affair and replaces the baked pot with an unbaked one. There is a storm and flooding. As the woman starts to swim, the pot melts away and she is swept away by the strong currents.

We ask the boys and girls, who is responsible for the girl's death? Who is right or wrong? Such a story gives us subtle ways of handling sexuality and morality concerns.

Boys and girls slowly take clearly opposite positions first and gradually understand the complexity of the situation.

Life Skills, Role-play and Discussion on Conflictual Situations

Life skills have been described extensively in the WHO documents.[9] The life skills and role-play activities were used especially with the older children to promote the following life skills:

- Critical thinking
- Creative thinking
- Decision making
- Empathy

---

[9] For further details refer to: Life skills documents by World Health Organisation and National Institute of Mental Health and Neurosciences, PB 2990, Bangalore.

- Communication skills
- Interpersonal skills, Self awareness
- Coping with emotions
- Coping with stress
- Problem solving

It has been observed by us that the tribal children were unusually high in pro-social behaviour and low in aggression. Even the teacher reports supported this observation. In the residential schools, the older children took good care of the younger ones. Pushing, shoving, teasing were seen rarely. When speaking to the adolescent boys and girls separately, we discovered them to be unable to communicate and negotiate with peers or adults for conflict resolution. We combined life skills approach using one situation to depict several conflict resolutions through negotiation and effective communication. Typically, we used three methods/situations. We have been able to:

- Discuss different points of view by different people
- Empathise with the situation the other person is in
- Communicating clearly to resolve the situation; understand that everyone has their own difficulties.

Developmental domains, which are dealt with, are:
Concerns of adolescents in the realms

- School performance and examinations
- Interpersonal difficulties with teachers, parents and peers
- Fears and anxieties about themselves
- Moral and sexual concerns

However, we have not objectively evaluated the effectiveness of our life skills programme. We believe that children found it useful. The teachers also found children to be more interactive.

EXCERCISES

Do Not Instruct: Always Encourage and Applaud.

STEP 1: Warming Up exercises

Drawing (art work)

- Craft work
- Singing
- Dancing
- Drama
- Storytelling
- Language games
- Number games
- Colour game
- Play

STEP 2: Find out what they already know.

STEP 3: Allow them TIME, SPACE, MATERIAL.

STEP 4: NOTE what you have discovered.

Summary

Play promotes motor, cognitive, language, emotional, social and moral development. Play includes games and any creative activity using activities such as art, craft, and language.

Sports and Games (Both Traditional and Regular)

Fine and gross motor skills

Visual and motor coordination

- Attention
- Quick reaction time
- Body balance
- Social – following rules and pro social behaviour
- Moral: against antisocial behaviour
- Problem solving
- Relaxation and enjoyment

Free Art and Craft

- Fine and gross motor skills
- Visual and spatial perception
- Use and understanding colours
- Communication of reality, fantasy, creativity and beauty
- Emotional expression
- Self-esteem and confidence

Language through word games, songs, stories, enactment, riddles and proverbs

- Attention
- Symbolic thinking
- Abstract thinking
- Problem solving
- Reality testing
- Self expression
- Communication with others

Reading (Top down)

Story with pictures>page>para>sentence>word>letter

Singing, Dancing and Drama

- Skills of movement
- Rhythm in movements and sounds
- Overcoming shyness and fear
- Expression of thoughts and feelings, learning by imitation

Number Work through games (identifying numbers, shop games), sticks and abacus number concept

- Concrete
- Semi concrete
- Abstract

What is Balavana Model of Learning?

Present School System Top Down	Balavana Model Bottom Up
Teacher Centred Teaching	Child Centred Learning

Syllabus Focused	Child Development Focused

Rote memorizing of 3Rs (reading, writing, arithmetic)	Holistic with activities
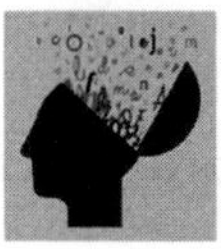	
 Burden on Teachers ↑	 Burden on Teachers ↓
Teaching aids with teachers	Learning and material owned by children

 Teacher is responsible	 Children are responsible
Teacher disciplines, punishes & criticises	Teacher supports, appreciates & encourages

Balavana Model Empowers the children

19

Pre-School Teachers or Play Home Staff*

IN THE urban areas there are pre schools which cater to young children below the age of 5 years to 10 months.

In the rural areas, Anganwadi workers have too many responsibilities. They are responsible for dealing with pregnant women and mother's health. They need to survey about health.

They also manage Anganwadi Kendras. These are not very easy tasks. They have to see to it that all the children below 6 years come to the Anganwadi every day. Occasionally food grains, utensils and water may not be available, but they are expected to provide meals for the children. They have to manage the Kendras in the surroundings of schools, houses, temples and Panchayat Kendras under these circumstances.

---

* The authors of this chapter are Malavika Kapur and Uma H.

In this chapter that can also be considered a manual, we deal with topics such as physical and mental health of the mother and child and suggestions regarding them are given in a simple way.

It is important to take care of the physical health of the pregnant women or women who has delivered the child. But it is equally important to take care of the psychological disturbances. The mothers may be depressed, may talk irrelevantly, get angry easily etc. Usually the family performs poojas and wait for the recovery of the person. For such problems, it is essential that she is taken to a psychiatrist and treated promptly.

In some other cases pregnant or nursing mothers get fits or seizures. They need to be attended to by the doctor in the primary health centre. If the fits reoccur several times they would affect the brain. Hence it is important that they are attended to by the primary health care doctors and under medication for five years. This applies equally to infants and children.

It is necessary that the pregnant women and women who have just delivered the babies have to be taken care of with love and affection. We need to understand their problems. With this, one can reduce their psychological disturbances. In our country the women who have delivered and the infants are given oil massage and bath. This is good for both mother and child. Breast feeding is good not only for physical health of the child, but also for mental development of the child. Breast feeding also helps bonding and development of affection between mother and child.

Child Development

All of us know that nutritious food is important for the development of a child. But what is to be provided for mental and intellectual development? Environment should be made conducive for play activity in children. Play is very important for children. Through play, a holistic development occurs in the children.

For Example: Give a small box to the child and observe how the child plays with the box. The child does not need factory manufactured and expensive play materials. Children pick up any available material and think, imagine and play with the same in different ways. Through such imagination and creativity, intellectual development occurs. In the same way when children at home and in the Anganwadi mingle with other children, they talk, sing, jump and play. Through all these activities their language ability, physical, psychological and social development occurs. They learn how to play with others without quarrelling. If children are not allowed to play and made to sit doing nothing, then their development gets impaired.

Responsibility of Preschool Teachers and Anganwadi Workers

It is good to allow children to play on their own. Care should be taken that children do not hurt themselves. When the children carry out any activity, they should be praised and encouraged. If children are scolded, beaten up, they in turn behave in the same way with the others. Love and affection from the mother and the care takers are very important for children. Thumb sucking, sleep talking are common in young children. There is no harm because of this.

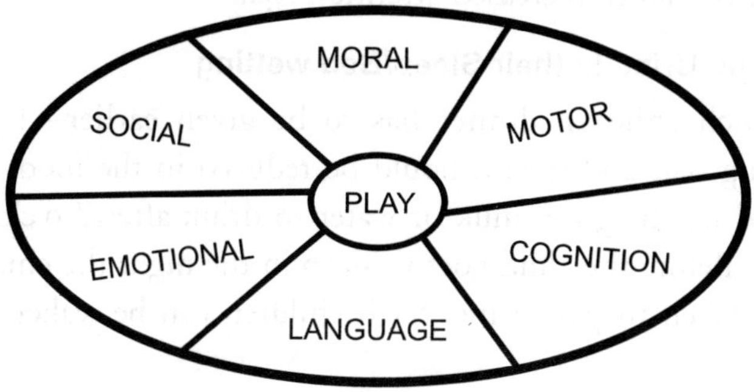

Mental Health Problems of Children

Some children are shy and fearful. Some children are quarrelsome. Some other children get angry quickly. Some children expect the things to be done exactly the way they want. With such children, if the adults behave the way the children want them to behave, children become even more stubborn. Sometimes children aged between 6 to 12 months, when they want something, cry so much that they hold their breath and go blue in the face. The adults get anxious about it. We might think that this is very dangerous for a child's life. But most of the time, what one is supposed to do is to distract attention of the child to something else. If it is done this way, stubbornness and temper tantrums would reduce.

Some children are overactive. They are always moving around. They do not sit quietly even for a few minutes. It is very natural for the young children to be active. The activity would decrease as they grow up. But if over activity (hyperactivity) is too much, then it needs treatment through therapy and medication. Their overactivity can be reduced by involving them in activities they like such as sorting out different coloured seeds or beads, stringing beads or flowers and sorting of different coloured and sized grains. Such activities in the beginning can be given for a short time and later the time duration can be increased. Children benefit from such activity and gradually activities lead to increased attention span.

Passing Urine in their Sleep/Bed wetting

For such children dinner has to be given earlier—by late evening, salt and spices should be reduced in the food. They should not be given milk or water to drink after 7 o'clock at night. Before the child goes to sleep in the night the child has to be taken to pass urine. Such children can be wakened up at night and should be taken to the toilet to urinate. With all these exercises the bed wetting decreases. When the children wet beds in their sleep, they should not be scolded, beaten or made fun of as these will only increase the problem. When the child has not wet his clothes, it is important to praise the child. Sometime, when the child who has been dry (toilet trained) starts wetting beds, the child may be having some fears or such other problems.

Learning Language

Some children learn language quickly, and some slowly. Such differences are common. But by 5 years all the children would have learnt one language. Even by 5 years if the child's pronunciation is not clear or if the child has stuttering or stammering, they have to be taken to a speech therapist. Children who have stammering should not be laughed at. They should be given more time and opportunity to talk.

Seizures/Epilepsy in Children

Epilepsy or 'fits' occurs in children of all ages. A typical fit may produce unconsciousness and convulsions. The fits occur always in the same manner. These are produced by abnormal electrical discharges in the brain. Consequently, they cause poor memory and difficulty in learning new material in the children if untreated. If the child has more than two fits he/she has to be kept on anti-epileptic drugs for five years without fail. Then the child can be fit free and lead a normal life.

Fits are not contagious, as it is commonly believed to be. If a child has a fit in your presence, please keep the child in a safe and airy place and do not do anything like restraining the child or stuffing the mouth with hard objects. The fits last only for a very short time. Take the child to the Primary Health Centre or to a Neurologist.

Physical Disability, Mental Retardation and Other Problems

For some children because of delayed development of the brain from birth, they may have physical disability, blindness, hearing impairment etc. There may be several reasons for this, for example: poor nutrition of the mother or the mother may have had some disease when she was pregnant. During or after the birth, if children are delivered with medical complication, the brain may be damaged. Parents of such children should be given training to stimulate the disabled children. Anganwadi workers can create awareness among parents and they themselves can provide stimulating environment for the brain development of the child.

For such problems, one should not spend too much of money on medicines, injection, prayer and pooja. One should start training and stimulation as early as possible. Though brain development may not happen rapidly, with persistence slowly the improvement will be seen. Thus tolerance, patience and trust are important, both for the families and those training these children.

If a child has physical disability, the child is to be given exercise to all the limbs of the body. Stimulation has to be given for hand, legs, neck and for balancing and standing. When child has polio or such other problem, the child has to be shown to the physician and their advice is to be taken. Free resources are available from the government which can also be utilised (Example: special type of supports, footwear etc.) Sometimes physical disability could be treated by surgery.

If the child has poor eyesight, the child has to be provided the spectacles. If other problems are identified regarding eyes, advise is to be taken from the eye doctor. If the child has some problem in the ears, the child is to be taken for check-up. The child may benefit from a hearing aid provided by the government (which can be free of cost).

If speech is delayed, one has to examine whether the child can hear properly. The Speech therapist needs to be consulted. Tongue has to be stimulated and also words and letters have to be taught over and over. The child has to be encouraged to look at the lips of the person who is speaking/teaching and learn from it. The child is to be taught to sit in front of the mirror and pronounce the words. Children can be taught words through pictures, games, drawings, common household objects, also from plants, trees and animals around.

If the child is mentally retarded, then the child has to be trained in all the areas mentioned above. Such children should be encouraged to play. They should not to be forced to read and, write. One should not compare them with other children and ridicule them. Children have to be encouraged in any activity they show interest in. For example: painting, reciting rhymes and poems, doing work.

When the child is not able to do its own activities (example: washing after toileting, wearing cloths, eating food), it is very important to give them the training. Training has to be given in a graded manner. Training should start from simple steps and then on to complicated levels. When the child is picking up a skill, for each step the child has to be praised. Along with the praise the child may be given eatables which the child likes. Through this, the child can be encouraged to learn skills.

Children who are disabled or have any other problems have to be taken care of with love and affection. If parents and Anganwadi workers train such children, as a grown up, the child will function independently and develop courage and self respect to some extent.

Government of Karnataka gives card and pension for all disabled children. With this, the child may get some benefits in future. For more information regarding this one can contact the village/taluk Tahsildar office.

Some Phases in a Preschooler's Life

- How well is the child attached to mother or the other adults in the family. If the attachment is insecure (too little, too much or anxiety provoking) the child will have difficulties in adjusting with strangers outside home or in preschool or nursery school or Anganwadi.
- At this age the child also learns to enjoy the company of other children, other than his/her own brothers and sisters. If he/she is too shy, too destructive, impulsive or aggressive, other children will refuse to play with such a child. It is necessary that the child is encouraged to be friendly and play with other children as an equal, without bullying, demanding the best or cheating. Some social rules have to be followed. Only child has often difficulties in mixing as an equal with other children.
- Child's self confidence is fragile. They need to be appreciated and not criticised. Comparing them with others is unfair and wrong. Comparison with other

children or the siblings produces anger and jealousy. It does not help the child in any way.

- Academic skills in a preschool stage, puts a burden on the child, which he/she is not ready for. Playing, storytelling, discussion of the stories, drawing, painting and answering their questions without tiring are the best methods to enhance their development.
- Talk to them about their emotions, relationships by asking them to describe the events in their daily lives.
- Do not hit or punish the child because you are angry. If the child needs to be disciplined, the reasons for it can be explained. The child can be deprived of your attention when he/she indulges in 'bad' behaviour.
- Television viewing for long and late hours is common in many Indian homes. Except for older children, most programmes including most cartoons are inappropriate for preschool children. Please give the children time to play, draw etc. and do not let them watch the television indiscriminately, Aggression and violence on television when seen by preschoolers, makes them more aggressive.

20

Dos and Don'ts for School Teachers*

Introduction

Teachers in India, especially in the Government schools in the urban and the rural areas, are expected to perform several tasks others than teaching. These tasks include:

- Collecting statistics of enrollment, attendance, dropouts to be submitted to the Block Education Officers
- Census enumeration
- Election duties
- Collecting text books and uniforms for the children
- Collecting rations to be given to the families once a month

* The authors of this chapter are Malavika Kapur and Uma H.

- Collecting rations and preparing and supplying mid-day meals in the government schools and in the Ashram schools
- Preparing and serving breakfast, lunch and dinner
- Supervising the washing, bathing, grooming and dressing of the inmates in the residential facilities
- Feeding all the children on a daily basis puts an enormous burden on the teachers in terms of time spent
- Attending teachers' meetings
- Attending teachers' training workshops organised by the education department
- Preparation of teaching aids
- Maintaining Health records of all the children and liaison with the PHC personnel
- Arranging community outreach programmes

Above all, the teachers are supposed to teach, conduct examinations and announce the results.

Understandably, attending to the large number of children in the class rooms with very poor infrastructure in the urban areas and in the single teacher multi-class primary schools in the rural areas is not an easy task for a teacher. The schools generally lack:

- Class room (in the rural area) or play ground space (in the urban areas)
- Furniture
- Stationery and books
- Drinking water
- Toilets
- Electricity
- Games and sports material
- Library and laboratory facilities

The Only resource we have in the schools are children. In view of the burden of work on the teachers and lack of infrastructure and facilities, there are other major problems. These are present in the children and teachers alike.

- Poor motivation
- Lack of interest
- Lack of commitment

This manual/chapter hopes to get around many of the problems by sensitising the teachers to some of the important aspects of teaching and learning and obstacles faced.

The areas covered are:

- Normal Child Development
- Psychological (mental health) problems which interfere with learning and adjustment
- Disabilities in children and mainstreaming in the class rooms

Normal Child Development

Normal development occurs from infancy through childhood to adolescence in the following areas:

- Motor
- Intellectual
- Language
- Emotional
- Social
- Moral
- Sexual

All the above areas are of concern to the children, parents and teachers. In the earlier decades of understanding of the child's mind, it was believed that the children are born with minds like 'clean slates' and that they learn everything from us. The current understanding based on the research in child development demonstrates that babies are born with enormous capacities of the brain and the mind to acquire skills soon after birth. We should not underestimate the ability of a baby to learn about oneself and others. Even a week-old baby can track objects with eyes, distinguish between the mother's face and a mask, even imitate some movements! They get bored with sameness in what they hear or see and shift their attention to something new. They come equipped to:

- Acquire motor skills (fine motor and gross motor)
- Understand the world (attention, observation, meaning, intelligence, including problem solving, analysis and synthesis and abstraction)
- Learn language and produce speech (Language)
- Feel emotions (Emotional)
- Relate to people (Social)
- Develop conscience (Moral)
- Sexual awareness (Sexual)

Of course, all these develop at a faster rate if the right kind of environment is provided. *Most babies are born equipped to start learning immediately*. It is worthwhile to remember that children can create their own world of learning, observing and picking cues from the environment. They observe carefully and imitate quickly whatever interests them; The development in all the seven areas mentioned above take place very rapidly in infancy, childhood and adolescence – then slows down.

Childhood is the best time for learning. If the statement supported by the research is true, **why do our children fail to learn?** Or is that they fail to learn in school, otherwise learn a lot from their environment, from observing, listening to stories and so on? Do the teachers try to find out what the children already know?

Most teachers believe that children can only learn when they are taught by their teachers. Often the children are compared to a lump of clay or an empty vessel which the teachers shapes or fills up. Teachers believe that they are the 'reservoir of knowledge' and the children are clean slates! Unfortunately, this attitude and belief is quite common amongst teachers and other adults. In this section on child development *we hope to persuade the teachers that all children come well equipped to learn about the world if given a chance.*

If given a chance, they can be skilled, creative, imaginative and communicative and demonstrate a new world of experience to the teachers. Children also come equipped with a temperament *(swabhava* or basic nature) like being shy, irritable, friendly, happy, active or dull. Some are very sensitive and some are not. Teachers often fail to note that the *children are different in their temperaments. The teaching and punishment methods used by the teachers are always the same.* Punishment, for example, may be viewed differently by different children. But praise makes them all happy (as in adults!) How does one create the right kind of environment for a child in the school to make him/her a good learner? The teacher has to reexamine his/her method of teaching. For example, the teacher draws on the black board a 'jug' or a 'fruit' asks the children to copy it. There is nothing creative in it. You are simply reproducing your lack of creativity as a teacher.

Instead why don't you try a different method? Give the children paper, pencil and colours (crayons/colour pencils) and tell the children to:

- Draw whatever you like
- Could be a flower, tree, person...
- School, village, market...
- Yourself, friends, family members...

In a class of 20 children you would get 20 different drawings. These may be different in

- Colour
- Content
- Size
- Beauty
- Expression of feelings/thoughts

Here it is the product of the child's own skills, thoughts, imagination, creativity and feelings. While the traditional approach permits you to find out only how well the child copies, the new approach permits you to explore the inner world of the child. You must understand that these drawings may not always be realistic, skillful or artistic. But it does not matter. It is a product of the child's inner world. It will improve with time and experience. In addition, you will note that the child enjoys this activity and does not get bored.

It will take a great deal of **inner discipline for a teacher not to tell** what the child should do. This applies equally to play, speech and any creative activity. The approach of discovering the joys of learning by the child himself or herself is not permitted in the standard teaching practices. For example, we teach by the method of instruction, which encourages imitation and rote learning (learning by heart). Children are made to copy elaborate scripts or alphabets endlessly for hours together. How can a child enjoy it? The task needs good gross motor and fine motor which a young child is yet to acquire. Copying the letters in a repetitive manner is indeed truly an IMPOSITION.

Instead, if you examine a letter of any script, you will note different shapes are incorporated in it. For example, circles, line, dots, triangles, strokes etc. A child can easily use these lines in a drawing drawn freely. For example, a sunrise behind the mountains with a tree and river in the front have all the strokes and lines to develop the child's gross motor and fine motor skills. Each drawing increases the skills of holding a crayon, a pencil or a brush. The child will joyfully learn the basic skills before starting to actually write.

Teachers often complain that children do not speak or answer questions. Sometimes the child may even have a mother tongue different from the medium of instruction. When the teacher expects an exact answer, the children are afraid that they do not know it. But when they play a word game like Anthakshari, they relax and are able to communicate – for example one can start with:

- Names of objects in the environment/picture
- Names of fruits, vegetables, animals
- Names of objects starting with a particular letter.

One can then go on to encourage the children to telling stories, to enact stories, to sing and dance.

Children can and will do these activities on their own, without being taught by the teacher. You will be surprised by their creativity if you give them a chance to experiment and be creative. We have through our research discovered that children can attain all the academic skills through art, craft, play, storytelling etc. Conventional teaching contributes very little to the overall development of the children while play-way child-friendly methods promotes overall development.

Though all teachers claim that they are familiar with 'joyful learning' methods in theory, they have no idea how it works – as they have not really witnessed it. If you could actually use these methods you will be surprised by creativity and learning skills of the children from disadvantaged populations such as slum children, scheduled caste and tribal children. According to the theories and practices of child development in the West and our own research with children in the government schools in urban and rural India, **we have no doubt that child-friendly methods – using the child as the resource can work wonders with our children in enhancing their overall development.**

Common Psychological Problems in Children

All children face some problems or the other as they grow up. These problems are to be considered a disorder – which needs to be attended to, only when:

- It has gone on **too long**
- It is **too severe** and **cannot be tolerated**
- It is **distressing** to the **child or those around or both**
- It **affects** the **school performance**

What are the Causes?

The problems may arise because of the **child** or the problems in the **child's environment.**

The child characteristics are:

- Child's temperament (too timid, aggressive, passive, restless, etc.) that he/she is born with
- Level of intelligence
- Sensory deficits (poor hearing, vision)
- Motor deficits (weakness of hands/legs or poor motor coordination)
- Mild or severe delays in development (motor and language)
- Chronic physical illnesses

The Environmental Contributors Are

Family:

- Parents who fight or are difficult

- Anxious, ambitious, over protective
- Indifferent or neglecting
- Excessively strict or punishing
- Sibling rivalry or jealousy

Social:

- Financial (poverty) and social problems (social class or caste or religion related)
- Neighbours of different social strata
- Gang of friends who are antisocial
- Children who do not mix socially

School:

- Problems may arise out of the poor school system, the teachers and the other children
- Teachers who like the parents may be neglecting, punishing or indifferent
- Teachers who do not teach and blame the infrastructure, children or due to personal problems

Children:

- Bully weaker and younger children or tease the girls
- Align with teachers and punish the children

Exclude children because they are of lower caste, poorer, girls or have disabilities.

Causes are Mostly Many and Not Single

For example, a child from a poor background being neglected at home, with no friends in the school or neighbourhood because of her shy nature may not do well in school, though she has an average intelligence. The teacher may consider her stupid and make fun of her. There are **many** causes to her poor school performance; that is within the child, at home and in the school. Another illustration is that of a poor home where the father drinks and beats the mother. The mother works as a coolie and supports the family. The family has three children. The elder boy is aggressive in school, fights a lot with other and does not study; the second boy has friends in school, studies well and is very popular among his classmates. The third one is a girl who is very quiet, worrying, anxious and preoccupied with the problems at home. She is not doing well in studies. All of them share the heredity and home and school environments.

Yet They Are So Different Why?

- The elder boy has inherited a difficult temperament and has learnt to imitate his father's behaviour.
- The youngest girl has inherited her mother's passivity and behaves in a similar fashion.
- The second boy has got good or resilient temperament, which has protected him from being influenced by a psychologically unhealthy home environment.

Common Psychological Problems of Childhood

These can be described as follows:

- Disorders in children may be seen as externally directed or internally directed problems. That is, it may be disturbing to the child or to the others or both.

Externalising or Conduct Disorder

(Behaviours which are disturbing to others)

In the very young children these may be seen as

- Overactivity
- Impulsivity
- Poor attention and distractibility

In the older child it may be manifested in:

- Stubbornness
- Temper tantrums

- Fighting
- Bullying
- Lying
- Stealing
- Destructive
- Disruptive
- Missing school deliberately

Internalising or Emotional Disorder

(Problems which are distressing to the child)

- Shyness
- Fearfulness
- Anxiety
- Extreme sensitivity
- Not having friends
- Quiet
- Withdrawn/sad
- School refusal
- Cries easily

Physical Symptoms Related to Stress

(When upset may have physical symptom)

- Stomach pain
- Headache
- Vomiting
- Asthma (wheezing attacks)
- Other body symptoms without physical basis

Developmental Delays

- Delayed or poor speech and language development
- Stammering and stuttering or articulation difficulties

It is important to observe whether the child understands the spoken language. Children differ in acquiring speech and language skills. Some attain them by one year. Another may speak clearly in the 5th year. Poor speech or pronunciation is common in the children below the age of six.

Stammering is due to faulty learning and can be treated. When any of the above persists, they should be referred to a speech pathologist.

Wetting and Soiling in the School or At Home

It is common for children to urinate frequently when:

- They are young
- Frightened
- Have weaker bladder control (runs in the family)

Teachers should not punish them but allow them to go to the toilet. One should not make fun or punish him when a child wets or soils himself or herself. It is not an illness, with some training the child will outgrow it.

Poor School Performance

Poor school performance may be due to

- Poor school system and faulty teaching practices
- Child having difficulties with the medium of instruction, having a different mother tongue
- Sensori motor handicaps
- Low intelligence
- Poor attention
- Home demands leading to irregular attendance
- Psychological problems described earlier
- Specific learning difficulties

Specific learning difficulties need a special mention. When the child has any of the above problems, and appears to have average intelligence, the child has only difficulties in **reading, writing and mathematics alone or in combination.** These children require remedial teaching, which involves preparing lessons of classes at a lower level at least 3 years below and building up the basic skills. The above problems are minor psychological problems of childhood.

What to Do?

With the Child:

- Listen to the child without interrupting
- Establish a relationship when the child feels free to relate to you by being friendly
- Take interest in the child's activities and feelings
- Find out what problems the child faces at home and school
- Encourage him/her to work on the possible causes for the problems
- Work on the possible and simple ways to solve the problems
- Focus on the child's special talents and achievements as it enhances the child's self esteem

In the School

If the problem lies within the school, teacher, other children or the studies (teachers, head master or other children).

- Negotiate with the others on behalf of the child
- Find out if the problem can be solved by talking to the parents

Epilepsy

Epilepsy or 'fits' occurs in the children of all ages. A typical fit may produce unconsciousness and convulsions. The fits occur always in the same manner. These are produced by abnormal electrical discharges in the brain. Consequently, they causes poor memory and difficulty in learning new material in the children if untreated. The best thing to do is get medical and professional help.

Class Room Management of Difficult Behaviours

- If the child is overactive, with poor attention, provide a quiet place and give simple tasks to improve attention like stringing beads or sorting grains by colour, shape or size. Praise each time he/she completes the task.
- If the behaviour is destructive, explain that the behaviour is unacceptable to the teachers as well as other children. If punishment is unavoidable: discuss first with the child and the other children and ask them advice an how this bad behaviour could be controlled. This always brings out suggestions and conforming to good behaviour by the children.
- Ignore and not pay attention to the disruptive behaviour.
- 'Time out' – send the child to a place where he does not get attention, a corner or a room. But it should be a minute per year of the age of the child. Not too long and not in dangerous places.
- Do not punish but praise generously.
- Group work with children can be held to discuss common problems encountered by them at school, home and within oneself.
- Problem solving exercises. For example, examining alternative solutions, discussing the advantages and disadvantages of each, to choose one and trying it out.

Problems of adolescence can be very difficult and needs to be handled differently. Some serious problems such as mental illness, depression and suicidal threats, addictions and sexually transmitted diseases may be the cause for concern in this group. However, masturbation, homosexuality and heterosexual interests must not be viewed as abnormal. These may be talked about as normal manifestations.

Concerns of the adolescents may be taken up in separate groups for the boys and girls. We have used life skills education, role play and open and non-threatening discussion of sensitive topics in the rural high schools. Sexuality should be discussed in the context of human feelings, relationships, values and societal expectations. Protected sex should receive attention.

Multiple Disabilities in Children and Mainstreaming

Children with disabilities could belong to any of the following categories:

- Intellectual retardation
- Visual impairment
- Hearing impairment
- Orthopedic impairment

The disabled children are issued identity cards if the disability crosses 50 per cent on a measuring scale. The 10-cards[10] enable them to obtain pension, travel concession, aids and appliances and job reservations later. It is good if the teachers are familiar with the procedure of obtaining the 10-cards if there are children with disabilities in the classroom.

The government ruling stipulates that the disabled should be mainstreamed in the schools. This is especially so in the rural areas, where the disabled do not have the opportunity to attend the special schools.

How Can Teachers Help the Disabled to Integrate in the Normal Schools?

- Teachers and the children should understand the problems faced by the disabled in the school setting. They could play the games where they can put themselves in the situation of not being able to see, hear or walk and understand what are the difficulties

[10] Disability identity card that provided ten types of assisstance.

in learning in the class rooms for playing with the other children.

- Make the teachers and other children appreciate the other skills the disabled have to develop to survive.
- Cultivate empathy by talking to the disabled children about their lives.
- Include them in all the activities as far as possible in the school and help them.
- Have a class room discussion on what it is to be different through stories role-play and dramas. For example, according the child given below:
    - Girl
    - Scheduled caste
    - Scheduled tribe
    - Disabled

Give a chance to the rest of the children to understand how discrimination of any sort hurts. However, it must be remembered that the teachers and the children can be unkind and cruel, unknowing or deliberately. These issues need to be resolved through open discussion with the sense of justice and compassion.

The child's world is simple, creative and joyful. Yet we as adults do not recognise these and cherish them, Instead we create a complex world with our own expectations, mindsets and deceptions and fails to recognise their individuality and respect them. Why the Hurry? Why can we not allow them play, share their joy and be happy when they are young?

References

1. Abrol U, Family and Child Welfare with Special Focus on Gender Bias. Paper presented in the Symposiums on New Directions in Human Development and Family Studies, MS University, Baroda, 1990.
2. Anagol J (2003). Compulsory Primary Education. Opportunities and Challenges. Booklet 2, Pune, Indian School of Political Economy.
3. ASER (2008-2017). Annual States of Education Report (Rural 2008).
4. Bailey SM (1994). Criminal Justice Matters, *The Psychologist* 7:6, 274.
5. Bloom K Social Elicitation of Infant Vocal Behaviour, *Journal of Experimental Psychology*, 1977, 23, 367-377.
6. Bowlby J (1980). *Attachment and Loss* (Volume 3). New York, Basic Books.
7. Centerwall BS (1994). Television and the Development of the Superego: Pathways to Violence. In *Children and Violence* (Eds) C Chiland and Young GT, Vol.2, *The Child in the Family*, NJ Jason Aronson Inc.
8. Chomsky, Noam (1965). *Aspects of the Theory of Syntax. MIT Press.*
9. Conradie DP, Heineke M and Botha MP (1987). The Effect of Television Violence on Television Naive Pupils. A follow up study over five years. Pretoria, *Human Sciences.*
10. Eron LD and Huesmann LR (1984). The Control of Aggressive Behaviour by Changes in Attitudes, Values and Conditions of Learnings. In *Advances in Studies ofAggression,* (Eds.) RJ Blanplank and DC Blanch and Orlando Fla, Academic Press, pp 139-171.
11. Ghosh S The Female Child in India – A Struggle for Survival. *Bulletin of Nutrition Foundation of India*, 8(4), 1987.

12. Gopnik A, Meltzoff A and Kuhl O (1999). *How Babies Think. The Science of Childhood*, London: Weidenfeld and Nicolson.

13. Harlow H, Nature of Love. *American Psychologist*, 1958, 13, 673-85.

14. Joy LA, Kimball MM and Zabrack ML (1986). Television and Children's Aggressive Behaviour. In *Impact of Television: A National Experiment in Three Communities* (Ed.) TM Williams, Orlando Fla, Academic Press, pp.303-360.

15. Kruttschnitt C, Heath L, and Ward D (1986). Family Violence, Televisioning Habits and Other Adolescent Experiences Related to Violent Criminal Behaviour. *Criminology* 24:2, 235-267.

16. Milavsky JR, Kessler RC, Stipp, H and Rubens W (1982). *Television and Aggression. A Panel Study* Orlando Fla, Academic Press.

17. Newson E (1994). Video Violence and Protection of Children. *The Psychologist* 7:6, 272-274.

18. US Commission on Causes and Prevention of Violence.

19. Oommen A, Kapur M and Sarmukaddam S (1987). Psychological Deficits Associated with Hyperactive Syndrome. *NIMHANS Journal*, Vol.5, pp.109-113.

20. https://www.aap.org/en-us/advocacy-and-policy/aap-health-initiatives/Pages/Media-and-Children.aspx?nfstatus=401&nftoken=00000000-0000-0000-0000-000000000000&nfstatusdescription=ERROR%3a+No+local+token

21. https://my.vanderbilt.edu/developmentalpsychologyblog/2014/04/effect-of-video-games-on-child-development/

22. http://www.npr.org/sections/ed/2016/01/06/461920593/kids-and-screen-time-a-peek-at-upcoming-guidance

23. http://www.pamf.org/parenting-teens/general/media-web/videogames.html

24. India (2009). A Reference Manual Completed by Research. Reference and training division, Chapter 10. Ministry of Information and Broadcasting, New Delhi.

25. James W (1980). *Principles of Psychology*. New York, Holt.

26. Jones CO (1988). Sexual Abuse. Fleeting Trauma or Eating Disorder (pp 515 – 527). In Anthony JE and Chiland C (Editors). Vol. 8. *Perilous*

Development: Child Raising and Identity Formation under Stress. New York. The Wiley Interscience Publication.

27. Kanner Leo, *Child Psychiatry* (1997). (4th edn) Springfield: CC Thomas
28. Kapur M 1995, 1997, 2011.
29. Kapur M and Mukundan H (2002). *Child Care in Ancient India from the Perspectives of Developmental Psychology and Paediatrics.* Delhi, Sri Sadguru Publications, Indian Books Centre.
30. Kapur M (2007). *Learning from Children What to Teach Them.* New Delhi, Sage Publications India Private Limited.
31. Kapur M (2016). *Psychological perspectives on child care in the Indigenous health systems,* New Delhi. Springer Private Limited.
32. Kynch J and Sen A Indian Women: Wellbeing and Survival, *Cambridge Journal of Economics.* 1983,7,363-380.
33. McWhirter L (1988). The Meaning of Violence for Children of Ireland. (pp 479–496). In Anthony JE and Chiland C, The Child in his Family, Perilous Development *Child Raising and Identity Formation under Stress.* Vol. 8. New York. Wiley Interscience Publication.
34. Milavsky JR, Kessler RC, Stipp H and Rubens W (1982). Television and Aggression. A Panel Study Orlando Fla, Academic Press.
35. NCERT (1987) (National Council for Education Research and Training).
36. Newson E (1994). Video Violence and Protection of Children. The *Psychologist* 7:6, 272-274.
37. NIPCCD (1987).
38. Ommen A, Kapur M and Sarmukaddam S (1987). Psychological Deficits Associated with Hyperactive Syndrome. *NIMHANS Journal,* Vol.5, pp.109-113.
39. Piaget J (1929). *The Child's Concept of World,* New York, Harcourt, Brace and World.
40. Priyavart Sharma (1963). *Charaka Samhita,* Banaras, Chaukhambha Oreintalia.
41. Rutter M and Cox A (1985). Other family influences. In Rutter M and Hersov L (Editors). *Child and adolescent psychiatry: Modern approaches* (2nd edition) (pp 58 – 81) Oxford. Blackwell Scientific Publications.

42. Rutter M (1989). Psychiatric Disorder in Parents as a Risk Factor for Children. In Schaffer D, Phillips I and Enzer NB (Editors). Prevention of mental disorders. Alcohol and other drug use in children and adolescents. OSAP prevention monograph, office of substance abuse prevention, US Department of Health and Human Services, Rockville, MD.

43. Sharma Y, Learning from Children What to Teach Them. In *Education Dialogue*, 2005, 2 (2), 273-75.

44. Tewari PU (2002). *Kashyapa Samhita.* Varanasi, Chaukhambha Vishwabharati.

45. US Commission on Causes and Prevention of Violence.

